Joyce Cary

By Kinley E. Roby

Northeastern University

Twayne Publishers · *Boston*

Joyce Cary

Kinley E. Roby

Copyright © 1984 by G.K. Hall & Company
All Rights Reserved
Published by Twayne Publishers
A Division of G. K. Hall & Company
70 Lincoln Street
Boston, Massachusetts 02111

Book Production by Marne B. Sultz

Book Design by Barbara Anderson

Printed on permanent/durable acid-free
paper and bound in the United States of
America.

Library of Congress Cataloging in Publication Data

Roby, Kinley E.
  Joyce Cary.

  (Twayne's English authors series ; TEAS 377)
  Bibliography: p. 128
  Includes index.
  1. Cary, Joyce. 1888–1957
—Criticism and interpretation.
I. Title. II. Series.
PR6005.A77Z784 1984 823'.912 83-18344
ISBN 0-8057-6863-7

Contents

Joyce Cary

Twayne's English Authors Series

TEAS 377

About the Author

Kinley E. Roby is Professor of English and department Chairman at Northeastern University and a field editor for G. K. Hall & Company. Professor Roby is the author of *The Writer at War: Arnold Bennett 1914–1918* and *The King, The Press And The People,* a study of Edward VII. Professor Roby's essays have been published in *Modern Fiction Studies* and other scholarly journals.

Preface

Joyce Cary is a fascinating and powerful novelist. Universal in the scope of its vision and solidly grounded in a belief in the fundamental brotherhood of man, his fiction presents a view of life that is at once exhilarating and terrifying. Viewed from Cary's perspective, the human potential for development is unimpeded by any divine sanctions, although, at the same time, humanity is condemned to live in a universe that is in constant flux. Life is a drama of endless opportunity and challenge which is played out against a constantly shifting background and which provides the narrative and psychological tensions of his art.

Cary's work is remarkably unified. His writing deepened and strengthened over the years without undergoing any significant change in focus or subject matter. From first to last, his subject, presented under various guises, is the unchangeable changeableness of life. His invariable theme is the force of that change.

Whether Cary's attention is focused on the catastrophic disruption of tribal life brought about by the arrival of the white man in a Nigerian village or on the fatality of Gulley Jimson's passionate involvement in his mythic visions, the narrative drive always originates from the onward rush of life burning in and often consuming the characters. The results of this forward motion are always the same: old structures are crushed and swept away, and those who oppose the change are frequently destroyed, innocent victims of the violence generated by the shattering changes.

In the consistency of his vision, Cary belongs to an ancient tradition in English letters, extending from William Langland to D. H. Lawrence and beyond; but he also differs from these writers in a very important respect. Like Arnold Bennett he refused to find a pattern in life. No vision of a moral order, immanent or transcendent, informs his writing. He sees no meaning in change. No malign or beneficent prescription commands his characters' lives. Man is chained in freedom.

Cary looks out from his novels and stories with a stoic resolve. No music accompanies the gyration of Cary's worlds. One hears only the crashing of walls and the confused sounds of the dying. Yet, Cary is not the apostle of despair. Quite the opposite; he is one of the greatest celebrators of life in our language, and he found beauty everywhere.

Robert Bloom has written at length in *The Indeterminate World* of Cary's refusal to take a moral stand in his fiction, suggesting that Cary's reputation has suffered as a consequence.[1] Other critics have also mistakenly found fault with Cary, as they did with Arnold Bennett, for failing to find meaning in life, for failing to forge from the material under his hands some beacon of hope to raise against the onset of darkness.

It is always sad when a good writer is neglected. And Cary is almost beyond question one of the greatest novelists of this or any other age. His skill in creating diverse and arresting characters is impressive. Aside from such memorable inventions as Gulley Jimson, Sara Monday, and Clerk Johnson, he has brought into being a whole town of characters. Moreover, it would be difficult to improve on Cary for richness and intricacy of plot. Incident abounds in his work. Settings are handsomely set forth and in great variety. He gives his readers a view of every level of late nineteenth- and early twentieth-century English society, not to mention his African work in which colonial and tribal life are presented with enormous power.

Although he wrote stories, early and late in his career, the bulk of his work lies in his novels, and it is on the novels that his fame deservedly rests. In the novels he deals with a variety of eternally relevant topics, such as the role of art and artists in modern life, women and their roles, the manifestations and consequences of religious commitment, and the ambiguities of political life, with its attendant issues of truthfulness and the nature of honor. Throughout his work he continuously explores the force of sexual love. In fact, love in all its forms absorbs him.

The present study deals primarily with Cary's fiction. However, because he considered his nonfiction to be an important part of the expression of his ideas and concerns, I have included a brief discussion of his books and essays on art, politics, and the issue of African independence.

It is my hope that what I have written about Joyce Cary will encourage others to read him. I also hope that I have conveyed my liking and admiration for Cary and his work. Most of all I hope that this book will make more accessible to the reader the work of a great and often complex artist.

Kinley E. Roby

Northeastern University

Chronology

1888   Arthur Joyce Lunel Cary born 7 December in Londonderry, Northern Ireland, son of Charlotte Louisa Joyce Cary and Arthur Cary.

1903   Enters Clifton College near Bristol.

1906   Goes to Paris to study painting.

1907   Leaves Paris for Edinburgh and enrolls in the School of Art.

1909   *Verses,* privately printed. Enters Oxford.

1912   Joins English Red Cross unit in Balkans.

1913   May, returns to England and enters the Nigerian Service, Northern Division, under Lord Lugard.

1915   April, enters Southwest African Field Force and is sent to northern frontier, east of Nafada.

1916   Marries Gertrude Margaret Ogilvie.

1917   April, son Arthur Lucius Michael Cary born.

1918   Second son, Peter, born.

1919   *Saturday Evening Post* buys first of Cary's short stories. Retires from colonial service.

1926   Third son, Tristram Ogilvie Cary, born.

1928   Fourth son, George Anthony Cary, born.

1932   *Aissa Saved.*

1933   *An American Visitor.*

1936   *The African Witch*; a Book Society choice.

1937   Father dies.

1938   *Castle Corner.*

1939   *Mister Johnson.*

1940   *Charlie Is My Darling.*

1941 *A House of Children* and *Herself Surprised.*

1942 Hired by the Ministry of Information to write a film script for *Men of Two Worlds*. *To Be a Pilgrim*.

1944 *The Horse's Mouth*.

1946 *The Moonlight* (published in the United States in 1947, but is a failure).

1948 *Herself Surprised* published in the United States.

1949 Wife dies on 13 December. *To Be a Pilgrim* and *The Horse's Mouth* published in the United States. Book of the Month Club chooses *The Horse's Mouth* as a "reserve selection." *A Fearful Joy*.

1951 Hospitalized with an undiagnosed illness.

1952 *Prisoner of Grace*.

1953 George Cary dies of heart disease. *Except the Lord*.

1955 Goes on a Greek lecture tour and is hospitalized on his return. *Not Honour More*.

1956 Norman Rosten's stage adaptation of *Mister Johnson* opens in New York to good reviews.

1957 Cary dies on 29 March.

1959 *Captive and the Free* published posthumously.

Chapter One

A Man of Courage: The Life

Arthur Joyce Lunel Cary was born on 8 December 1888 in Londonderry, Ireland. On his father's side he was a member of the once flourishing Anglo-Irish landowning Carys of Inishowen Peninsula who had lived on their rocky and mountainous lands since the days of Queen Elizabeth. Forced to abandon their heavily mortgaged estate by Gladstone's Irish Land Act of 1882, which canceled the rent arrears of their tenants, the family had scattered; but Joyce Cary's father, Arthur Pitt Chambers Cary, set himself the task of redeeming the family's fortune.[1] He went to London to study engineering and returned to Ireland to marry Charlotte Louisa Joyce.

Charlotte Joyce, the daughter of James Joyce, a Belfast bank manager and prominent Derry business man, was a popular choice for Arthur Cary. The marriage of the two caught the imagination of Londonderry and became a civic event, linking an old Anglo-Irish landowning family to a thriving Irish mercantile family.[2] County Connemara, where the couple settled, is Joyce country, and Joyce Cary's choice of the name Joyce over Arthur or Lunel suggests a conscious identification with his Irish inheritance. But Cary's stay in Ireland was of short duration. His father soon moved the family to London, where a collection of uncles and aunts formed an exiled Cary tribe in the city.

The first direct blow that Cary experienced in his life was the death of his mother in 1898, when he was ten years old. Already a withdrawn child, nearly blind in his right eye and suffering from various ailments, his loss drove him further into himself, making him a confirmed bookworm. His father's youngest sister, Netta, took over the family, and her powerful, independent personality deeply impressed the sensitive nephew, who came to love her and feel close bonds of affection between them. As for his mother, there is reason to believe that he never forgave her for dying and leaving him, and her death had a lasting effect on his writing.

1

Cary's favorite childhood experiences were connected with Ireland, where his grandmother Cary lived at Clare Cottage in Inishowen or with his mother's family at Ravenscliffe.[3] There was swimming in Lough Foyle and sailing and a wild surrounding hill country in which to wander and play the long summer days away. *Castle Corner* and *A House of Children* capture this world in vivid and loving detail. But the country was even then in the throes of political turmoil, and in his Irish summers Cary saw men fighting and felt the deep divisions that were sundering Irish society.

In 1900 Arthur Cary remarried, and in the fall of the same year Cary and his brother, Jack, age six, were sent to Hurstleigh School in Tunbridge Wells. Jack was a good athlete, but Cary was not. Neither was he a particularly talented student. Joyce spent three undistinguished years at Hurstleigh and was sent to Clifton College in 1903.[4] The move was no improvement for Cary. Clifton was strong on sports and prepared its students for the great military colleges. Cary's poor eyesight and weak health unfitted him for sports, and he had no interest in military matters. Instead, he enjoyed telling stories and drawing pictures.

In the spring of his first year at Clifton, his stepmother, Dora Stevenson Cary, died of pneumonia. It was another serious loss to Cary, who had developed a strong attachment to his stepmother. In his grief he ran away from Clifton, to reach his father; but the school authorities managed to have him caught at Paddington Station and returned to Bristol. Arthur Cary wrote his son a letter, encouraging him to be brave and not to add to his father's burdens. From then on Cary bore the loss of his second mother with stoical resignation.

The next major development in Cary's life came in 1906 when he completed his study at Clifton and persuaded his father to allow him to go to Paris to study art. For a year Cary enjoyed himself in Paris and Etaples on the coast south of Boulogne, drawing, meeting other art students, and sampling bohemian life. Then he met a Scottish artist, Charles Mackie, who persuaded him to go to Edinburgh and to take up the serious study of art.

Cary left Paris for Edinburgh in 1907 and enrolled in the Board of Manufacturers School of Art. For a year he worked diligently at mastering the basics of drawing and began to work with oils. He also began writing bad poetry. In his second year in Edinburgh, he had a volume of poems privately printed. *Verses,* as the book is titled, was dedicated to his father and signed Arthur Joyce. Foster is probably correct in surmising that Cary, who had been called Joyce since childhood, was seeking to flatter his father by using his name.[6]

Cary's reason for ingratiating himself with his father was that he now wished to abandon painting and take up literature. Although the poems were of poor quality, Arthur Joyce was impressed with his son's efforts and, perhaps in desperation, agreed that Cary should enter Oxford for the purpose of taking a degree in law and preparing himself to become a writer.

Cary passed the entrance examinations and entered Trinity College in the fall of 1909. The Oxford years were rich in experience for Cary. Here he met and became friends with John Middleton Murry, forming a connection that the critic, Barbara Fisher, regards as being of major importance in Cary's later life. He also met Gertrude Ogilvie, whom he later married.

Cary began his years at Oxford with adequate dedication to his studies, but as the months passed the appeal of work diminished. He became far more interested in his friends and in holiday excursions than in preparing for the examinations which would conclude his Oxford experience. When the examinations were given, Cary was totally unprepared. He sat for them and took a fourth, a pass so low that he was effectively cut off from the civil service and from teaching. He had utterly failed to prepare himself for entrance into any of the professional careers requiring a university degree.

In the face of this disaster, Cary went to London, determined to become a novelist; but he soon abandoned this second experiment with bohemian life in favor of something more exciting. The Montenegrans had gone to war against Turkey, and Cary made up his mind to have a firsthand look at the fighting. He remained with the Montenegrin army until May 1913, serving in the Red Cross and collecting notes for what became *Memoirs of the Bobotes,* an account of the war written shortly after his return home.

Cary's next move was to enlist in the Nigerian Service. He was posted to northern Nigeria in 1913 as an assistant district officer. But he had scarcely become accustomed to the country and come to grips with his job when war was declared. Drafted into the West African Frontier Force, he was posted to the Cameroons, but not before being slightly wounded by German rifle fire at Mount Mora on the northern frontier.

In the spring of 1916 he was sent home on leave and persuaded Gertrude Ogilvie to marry him. Returning to Africa, he completed his service, was discharged, and took up his duties again in the colonial service. Until 1920, when he resigned from the Nigerian Service, he saw his wife only on his occasional leaves. In 1917 his first son, Arthur, was born and a year later, Peter. As his letters testify, separation from his wife and young family was a severe strain on Cary.

During his years in Africa he again made up his mind to become a novelist and began to write voluminously. Short stories and segments of novels poured out, but he finished almost nothing he began, so that despite the piles of manuscript pages that accumulated, he had nothing to offer a publisher. It was in this period that he began the lifelong practice of beginning a novel, setting it aside to start another, and continuing until he might have as many as seventeen books in progress. He also read voraciously in English and European fiction. In particular he read Tolstoy and the other Russians.

Just a month before his 1920 leave, he sent several short stories to an Oxford friend, who had set up as a literary agent. The friend had offered the stories to the *Saturday Evening Post,* where three of them were accepted.[7] This success convinced Cary that he had a future as a commercial writer. He returned home and resigned his commission in the Nigerian Service. He bought a house on 12 Park Road in Oxford and settled down to become a full time novelist and short story writer.

Cary's euphoria lasted only through the summer of 1920. In the fall the *Post* rejected his most recent submissions as being too literary. He found himself unable to sell his stories and was thrown back on his and his wife's small private incomes. Living under great financial restraint and wearing emotional tensions, brought on by worry and a sense of guilt and failure, Cary and his wife managed to hold onto their house in Oxford and to keep Cary writing. As the decade advanced, they were eased somewhat in their finances by help from his wife's father, but it was to be many years before the shadow of financial strain was finally lifted.

In 1932 Cary finally managed to complete one of his novels, offer it for sale, and have it accepted. His first published novel was *Aissa Saved,* a story set in Africa. This success was followed a year later by another African novel, *An American Visitor.* Cary was now launched as a writer. Three years later he published *The African Witch.* From then on until the end of his life, he brought out something nearly every year.

In 1939 Cary made two unsuccessful efforts to widen his scope as a writer. The first endeavor was the result of an appeal from the Liberal Book Club, organized by George Orwell, to write a book of political theory offering an alternative to the extreme positions of the political left and right.[8] The book appeared under the title *Power In Men* and sold poorly, in part because of the outbreak of war and in part because of the bad editing job that had been done on the book.

His second try was with a stage play. Like Arnold Bennett before him, who had more success at it than Cary, Cary cherished the hope of becoming a successful playwright. His first effort, *The King Is Dead, Long live The King,* was an unqualified failure. Joseph Priestley, himself a successful playwright, read the script and told Cary to scrap it and start over. This he did but without any satisfactory results, and he abandoned the play as a bad job.

Having been rejected in his attempt to enlist, Cary remained in Oxford and served in the Civil Defense. Then, in 1942, he became involved in a Ministry of Information scheme to produce films to boost military and civilian morale and increase the war effort. In January 1943 Cary went off to Africa to serve as scriptwriter for the film, which was finally made in Tanganyika. The fact that Cary had absolutely no knowledge of films when his assignment began seems not to have been any hindrance. The film, *Men Of Two Worlds,* was made and apparently served its purpose.

In 1942 Cary also won the James Tait Black Memorial Prize for *A House of Children.* The prize led to an invitation from Edinburgh University to give an informal talk. Cary spoke on "Tolstoi on Art And Morals."[9] His trip was a great success in at least three ways. His talk was well received, he had an opportunity to meet many old friends from the days when he had been studying art in the city, and, finally, on the way back to Oxford he had the germ of the idea from which *The Horse's Mouth* came into being. During his time in Africa he wrote furiously on *The Horse's Mouth,* which was published in 1944, bringing the first trilogy to completion.

Cary continued to write and enjoy the benefits of his increasing financial security. By 1945 the war in Europe was drawing to a close, giving Cary and his wife hope of taking a holiday together, something they had been looking forward to for many years. But the Ministry of Information appealed to Cary to undertake another project. This time they needed a propaganda film that could be used to win support for England's continuing presence in India.

During the 1940s the Indian people had become increasingly restive under colonial rule and were demanding self-determination. Joyce was asked to do the script for a film set in northern India that would illustrate to the Indian population the benefits of an English-sponsored flood control and irrigation project. The project involved his traveling to India without his wife. Gertrude was very disappointed at being left behind and wrote to her husband to say that she did not think she could stand many more separations. There had already been too many of them in their married life. The film was, in fact, never made.

Cary returned to England to the good news that *The Moonlight* was to be published in the United States by Harper. But news of an entirely different character robbed his achievement of much of its gratification. His wife had developed cancer, and did not respond to treatment. An extensive operation in 1948 failed to arrest the disease. Despite brief periods of remission, the cancer advanced and led to her death in December 1949.[10]

A painful irony in Cary's life is the fact that after his wife's death he began to have an income from the sales of his books that would have allowed them to travel as much as they wished. His first major effort to express his new life was a trip to the United States, planned as a combination lecture tour and holiday. He left England in January 1951 and returned in April, at the end of a successful three months of journeying that carried him from New York to Los Angeles. The tour did a great deal toward restoring his energy and sense of purpose.

In the early 1950s Cary's publisher, Michael Joseph, decided to publish a uniform edition of his work. Cary was pleased, but it meant a great deal of work for him, because he was invited to prepare prefaces for the edition. He chose the name Carfax for the edition and toyed with the idea of writing a general introduction under the title "The Comedy of Freedom."[11] The Carfax Edition, named after the tower in Oxford's center, was eventually provided with a series of "Prefatory Notes" to the several volumes instead of a general introduction.

Reviewing the novels and writing the notes made him eager to express himself on the subject of writing. In this period he wrote three important essays on fiction writing—"L'Art" and "A Novel Is A Novel Is A Novel" for the *New York Times Book Review* and "The Way A Novel Gets Written" for *Harper's*. He also appeared on the BBC authors series and was interviewed by Lord David Cecil. The text of the interview was later published in the *Adam International Review*.[12] Cary had become a writer recognized on both sides of the Atlantic. Although the recognition was late in coming, Cary enjoyed it.

He continued to write and lecture at a fast pace, and turned again to the short story. In 1945 he had published an African story, "Bush River," in *Windmill* magazine. From then until the end of his life he continued to turn out occasional stories, the best of which were about children and Africa. He went regularly to Stratford to participate in the Shakespeare Festival, and made occasional forays onto the Continent to give lecture tours or merely holiday alone or with his family. Still, he found life without his wife difficult, not only because he was often lonely but also because he either could not or would not learn to cope efficiently with the house and with his manuscript preparation. A string of secretaries came and went.

In 1953 George, his youngest son, died of heart disease at the age of twenty-five. It was not a surprise. The surprise had been that George had survived infancy, but, of course, Cary felt the loss. George had been a remarkably fine student, winning a Double First in classics at Cambridge when he was only twenty.[13] George's death increased Cary's uneasiness and irritability, a state of mind that was reflected in his attacks in and out of print against the income tax authorities and those in favor of any form of censorship of books.

In 1951 Cary had not felt well and had consulted a doctor without any diagnosis being offered. In addition to his general feeling that he was not quite well, he developed what was generally thought to be bursitis. One leg dragged slightly and he had a certain amount of pain. By the spring of 1955 he submitted once more to examinations. He had planned a second American tour and was obliged to cancel it because of his poor health. Finally, in November of 1955, his illness was diagnosed as amyotropic lateral sclerosis. There was no cure for the condition, which would inevitably result in the gradual atrophy of the nervous system and the muscles, resulting in paralysis and death.[14]

For a time he was able to carry on his working routine as he had been doing, but after a fall on the attic stairs, he gave up his study on the top floor of the house and worked in his sitting room instead. As the disease progressed, he had handles fixed into the walls of the house to help him move from room to room, and sometimes he used a chair as a walker.[15] Cary confronted his illness with great courage. He became more and more determined to complete the work he had mapped out for himself and worked furiously at his writing. He had his religious trilogy still in hand, a dramatization of *Mister Johnson,* being carried out by Norman Rosten, and work connected with Andrew Wright's study, *Joyce Cary: A Preface to his Novels,* then in its planning stage. He was also preparing his Clark Lectures, which were published posthumously as *Art and Reality.*

When he could no longer write, even with the help of the mechanical contrivance that he had had constructed to steady his hand as he guided his pencil across the page, he dictated. Then, at last, he could not even whisper. His work was done. Although his body failed, his mind remained alert, and it was only at the very end, when the pain had become too great to bear, that he was finally sedated. In those last weeks he had been able to finish *Art and Reality* and two short stories, "Period Piece" and "The Sheep." He had given up work on *The Captive and the Free* four months earlier, aware that he would not have the strength to complete it. Cary died on 29 March 1957.

Chapter Two
The Emerging Artist

Few artists ever served a harsher apprenticeship than Joyce Cary. Between the sale of his last story to the *Saturday Evening Post* in the summer of 1920 and the submission of *Aissa Saved* to the publishers in 1931, Cary wrote incessantly, completing only one of the dozens of novels with which he struggled in those years. Until he succeeded in finishing *Aissa Saved,* none of the books on which he worked met his severe standards of excellence. But during these grim eleven years of labor, Cary gradually developed a consistent point of view and a technical method that became the basis of his art. How his ideas and his technique emerged and finally merged is the subject of this chapter.

When Cary discovered that he could no longer interest the *Post* editors in his stories, he was faced with a painful choice, either to return to writing the sort of commercial material the popular magazines demanded, or to follow his developing style wherever it might take him. In a sense the choice was made for him, because he found that he could no longer write the kind of story the *Post* wished to print. Cary had outgrown the restrictions of that kind of tale and felt compelled to push on.

At about the same time that he was losing his popular markets, he made a second alarming discovery. He felt that he lacked a comprehensive vision of life that would enable him to write the kind of book he wished ultimately to write. He had glimpsed the problem as early as 1916 when his efforts to teach himself to write were going badly and he was writing letters full of depression, even despair, to his wife. Now he saw the problem with absolute clarity, and his response was to begin spading up his life, as he expressed it, for the purpose of examining its foundations. He reached some fundamental conclusions about life, which became the supporting structure on which all of his later fiction was based.

In an interview Cary once insisted that he had a "clear and comprehensive idea of the world" he was writing about. He meant, of course, that he had a perception of reality and had found a way of living with it. His novels all deal with the complications, dilemmas, joys, and agonies the real world presents to its inhabitants as opposed to the imagined happiness that their fantasy worlds offer them. The basis of his vision was, in his own words, his realization of the "fundamental injustice of the world." He further observed that having experienced such an insight, one never recovered and had all subsequent thought colored by it. This observation makes comprehensible his comment that he had sought diligently to discover why "all men do not cut their throats." His fiction, from first to last, is an effort to answer the question.

The English novelist Enid Starkie, who knew Cary well and counted herself a friend and an admirer, expressed her conviction that Cary's idea of the world was not the effervescent, optimistic, and yea-saying one that has often been wrongly associated with him. She points out that there was in Cary's character a fundamental sadness, stemming not from the death of his wife, as has sometimes been suggested, but from some "earlier time,"[1] presumably a reference to Cary's perception of the "fundamental injustice of the world."

Starkie suggests that as a personality Cary was much closer to the conservative Thomas Wilcher in the first trilogy than to the explosive Gulley Jimson, with whom Cary has often been identified. To see Cary as an embodiment of optimistic and bustling energy is simply to ignore the violence, high incidence of failure, and collapse of hopes and dreams that haunt his fiction. Because of Gulley Jimson's dynamism and the swiftly accelerating action in the novel, it is easy to forget that Gulley's efforts to translate his dreams into art all more or less fail.

In 1914, when Cary sailed for Nigeria, he had behind him a volume of bad poetry and an uncompleted manuscript of a novel of student life in Paris that Middleton Murry remembers Cary working on while at Oxford. From the time of his entering the colonial service until his marriage in 1916 he did no further writing, although his letters of the period suggest that he was still thinking about it. From his marriage and his subsequent return to Nigeria, he began to reconsider seriously the possibility of becoming a writer. In a letter to his wife he wrote that he wished he had "had the courage years ago to defy all conventional notions of respectable living & write, write, write, for whatever I could make by it, even nothing."[2] Marriage and the prospect of becoming a father reawakened Cary's muse, not eagerness for fame.

Delayed as the new beginning was, Cary, once started, worked hard and fast. In September 1916 he wrote to Gertie to say that he had completed the first draft of a novel. Foster describes this stage of development as one in which Cary was "consciously mechanical, for he was learning about structure and pace."[3] The novel was being written in the first person and proving difficult. Cary finally abandoned the novel in disgust and did not attempt a first-person narrative again until *The Horse's Mouth.*

Cary's letters to his wife provide a skeleton account of the progress of his work; other sources add information of greater interest. From the unpublished manuscripts in the Cary Collection at the Bodleian Library, it is possible to see that during his apprenticeship years Cary developed a method of keeping ten or a dozen novels going more or less at the same time. It has been argued that this system was a consequence of Cary's early training as a painter and his familiarity with painters' methods of having several canvasses under development simultaneously. Another reason was Cary's remarkable fertility. Ideas and impressions, characters and situations crowded his mind. Rather than risk losing them, he wrote them down, sometimes in notes running to several thousand words. Many of these fragments later found their way into his novels and short stories.

Cock Jarvis, the protagonist of an early, incomplete novel, who appears in *Castle Corner* and again in later novels as a minor figure, is just such a "fragment." Cary worked on the Cock Jarvis novel from 1924 to 1937, accumulating about half a million words of copy without managing to create a satisfactory vehicle for his remarkable character.[4] In a rueful surrender Cary finally abandoned the novel in what he called "massive ruins." A. G. Bishop sorted through and arranged a selection of the two thousand pages of manuscript, which he published in 1976. The result is a version of the novel, but it remains fragmentary and is unsatisfactory.

Cary thought highly of the book, and asserted late in life that some of his best writing was to be found in its pages. In his foreword to *Cock Jarvis,* Walter Allen describes Jarvis as Cary's quintessential character, the Cary man. He also suggests that all of Cary's later writing flowed from his struggles to express Cock Jarvis as "the hallmark of Cary as a novelist, the character who is unlike the hero of any other English novelist . . ." (*CJ,* xiv). Cary's perception of Jarvis changed as he developed as an artist. He finally went beyond Jarvis but never finished with him.

After 1916 Cary decided to divide his creative energies between what he chose to call commercial and serious fiction. He settled on the short story as his commercial medium and the novel as his more serious concentration. He adopted the pen name Thomas Joyce to attach to his short stories, reserving Joyce Cary for the books that he hoped would establish his name as a serious novelist. For several years he kept his two efforts separate. As an average, on trek or in camp, whether working beside a camp fire or in the comparative luxury of a station bungalow, he turned out twenty thousand words of fiction a week, writing at the end of long exhausting days in an enervating climate.

He also wrote his almost daily letters home to his wife, providing Gertie with a running account of his days and his writing. Frequently depressed by what he considered to be the poor quality of much that he had written, he was plagued by a sense of having nothing to say, although he was never at a loss for incident or character. To ease his mind, he began to read English and European novelists, Balzac, Hardy, Conrad, Thackeray, and Tolstoy among them.[5] The company of such minds helped him to fight off loneliness and provided him with inspiration. But he was cut off completely from constructive criticism, his sensitivity and shyness preventing him from showing his work to anyone, including his wife.

In 1917 Cary again became a civilian official in the service and was assigned to a post in the Borgu Division of Nigeria. He began at once to write and, in the course of the next eight months, produced the equivalent of three novels. But this immense effort yielded nothing that Cary thought worth saving. Receiving word from headquarters that he was to be relieved, he burned everything he had written while in Borgu.[6] This wholesale destruction of material suggests that Cary's problems with his writing were more than technical in nature: something was profoundly wrong.

Part of the problem may have been created by the quinine he was taking to treat his malaria. In a 1917 letter to his wife, Cary complained that his bad memory was "worsened" by quinine and that he was made an "ignoramus" by it.[7] Apparently Cary was in despair over his writing, ill with malaria, and worn down by work. This state of dejection seems to have triggered the destruction of his manuscripts, but burning what he had written was something he never again repeated. In later years he would keep everything. He once told Andrew Wright that there were twenty-three novels in his attic in various stages of development.

Following a leave of absence, Cary returned to Africa with a stiffened resolve to get on with the writing, promising his wife in a letter that although he had destroyed last year's writing, he would not do so with this year's. He said that, in particular, he had two novels he was "burning" to get at again, and that the one he was currently working on was going very well.[8] Reading few novels, aside from some much-admired Jane Austen, Cary was now spending his spare time with Hazlitt, Plutarch, Darwin, and Sir Thomas Browne. These heavyweights tended to make him aphoristic, and he took to writing such things as "Art should not aim at explaining life but making it worth living."[9]

Writing very swiftly now, he started story after story without ever completing one, because he was struggling with technical problems of writing. In particular, he could not bring plot and characterization into line. He complained to his wife that as soon as he got his characters sufficiently differentiated, they ceased to evolve the plot and fell to struggling with it.[10]

At the same time he became concerned that his style was not what it ought to be, that it was not sufficiently under control. He thought that he alternated between being too florid and too sparse, too lavish in color and too monochrome.[11] He had promised his wife that he would work faithfully on one novel and complete it. His resolve lasted three weeks. In the previous year he had begun twenty novels without completing one of them. When he returned to England in 1918, he had yet to finish one.

First Success

Then in 1919 Cary wrote home that he had completed some short stories intended to be potboilers. He planned to offer them for sale. Through an old Oxford friend turned literary agent, Cary submitted several of his short pieces to the *Saturday Evening Post*. The *Post*'s editors promptly bought three of them for two hundred and forty pounds.[12] This success, coupled with a poor report on his physical exam, taken during the 1919 leave, made up his mind. He retired from the Nigerian Service and in 1920 bought a house in Oxford at 12 Parks Road.

The stories which had caught the editors' fancy were set in Paris rather than Africa, and were made up, as Joyce expressed it, of "a little sentiment, a little incident, and a Surprise," a formula O. Henry found had a magic quality. Through the spring of 1920 the *Post* continued to buy Cary's stories at a rate of nearly two hundred pounds each.[13] Cary saw all of his hopes for financial security coming to a swift fruition. Filled with creative zeal, he began work on a novel, setting apart one portion of each day for serious writing on it and keeping an absolute division between the Thomas Joyce potboilers and the fiction on which his fame was to rest.

This period of intense happiness was brought to a swift and painful end in the autumn of 1920. The *Post* suddenly rejected his stories, finding them too literary. Despite his efforts, he had not been able to keep his two kinds of writing separate. Struggling with style and plot and characterization in his novel, seeking to find a theme of sufficient worth to justify his effort, Cary allowed the struggle to enter his short stories. They lost their spontaneity, began to develop ideas, and ceased to be purely amusing. The change was fatal to their commercial appeal. The summer of 1920 brought his story selling to an end, except for an occasional acceptance by the *Strand Magazine,* until he experienced a resurgence of interest in the form in the 1950s. His hopes for early financial success were utterly dashed.[14]

Fred Ogilvie, Cary's brother-in-law, urged him to try writing a potboiler novel that would make some money. Joyce refused and his wife backed him in his decision. Foster writes that she felt Cary compromised himself enough in writing the short stories.[15] With the success of such writers as Maugham, Knoblock, Shaw, and Barrie to give him courage, he turned to drama instead and began, unsuccessfully, to work on a play called *Pru* or *Prudence.*[16]

At the same time Cary continued to write short stories and send them to English and American magazines, which rejected them. He also kept at his serious fiction, devoting a substantial part of every day to writing. In "The Novelist At Work" he wrote that at this time and for nearly ten more years he was stuck for "the want of a satisfactory general idea." Throughout the 1920s he began novel after novel, probably to the number of several dozens.[17]

Cary's manner of working on *Cock Jarvis* in these early years is, probably, a fair representation of his general method of work and reveals an approach that was to become standard with him. Between 1924 and 1926 he appears to have written "many different versions" of the story without finding one that satisfied him. For two years he experimented adventurously with character, plot, and theme, and then set the work aside in disgust (*CJ,* xv). In 1927 he completed what Bishop has called the definitive version of the story, but he remained unable to complete it. Repeated revisions followed over the next seven years.

The African Novels

With publication in 1932 of *Aissa Saved,* Cary began a series of African novels which was completed in 1939 with *Mister Johnson. Castle Corner,* published in 1938 with a chiefly Irish setting, breaks the continuity of this group of novels but is linked to the African novels by the appearance of Cock Jarvis, who conquers an African province. *An American Visitor* and *The African Witch* complete the list of Cary's African novels.

In the prefatory essay to *Aissa Saved* Cary records that, at the time of writing the novel, he was just breaking out of a "confused, foggy, disintegrated state of feeling and thought into moderately clear going."[18] This struggle produced in its first stages a novel of great length, bearing a heavy cargo of philosophical discussion. On rereading it Cary found the book boring and began to rewrite it. Over a period of three years he did several revisions, each aimed at further simplification.

In 1932 Cary published *An American Visitor.* Unlike *Aissa Saved,* which was an exploration of religious experience and had taken Cary four years to write, this novel emerged from Cary's obsession with Cock Jarvis. District Officer Brewsher is not exactly like Jarvis, but he does represent an attempt to deal with the Jarvis dilemma. The American woman, Marie Hasluck, originated in Cary's experience with an American woman in England who insisted that her five- and six-year-old children make their own moral decisions without any interference from herself. The prospect first alarmed and then intrigued Cary, who converted his curiosity into a novel.

With the publication of *An American Visitor,* Cary found his stride. *The African Witch* followed, then *Castle Corner,* with African episodes, and, finally, in 1939 *Mister Johnson,* Cary's greatest achievement with his African materials. The Nigerian junior clerk, on whom Johnson is based, was stationed in a quiet inland village and wrote letters home to his family on the coast. It was wartime and Cary was a military censor, among other things, compelled to read all letters originating in the interior, a militarily sensitive area. The letters contained romantic exaggerations of danger, excitement, and command which the young clerk had imagined. To these impressions, Cary added his experience with another African clerk who had stayed up all one night copying over a botched report in order that Cary might submit it on time and not "catch trouble." These and other impressions of African character combined in Cary's imagination to form the unforgettable and immensely dynamic *Mister Johnson.*

Taken together, Cary's African novels show a distinct method that, with minor changes, was to become the formula for all of his novels. Beginning with lived experiences, Cary brought to his memory of actual events the ferment of his thoughts and subjected the whole to a thorough scrutiny. Increasingly his method was to present dramatically through his characters and their actions all of the alternatives of conviction, persuasion, and, ultimately, action that the situation could generate. In a particularly revealing sentence and one that shows Cary's interest in his method, he describes Johnson as swimming "gaily on the surface of life . . . as all of us swim, with more or less courage and skill for our lives."[19] Cary hoped to create an experience for his readers that would persuade them, at least while immersed in one of his fictions, to do the same.

Chapter Three
The African Adventure

Between 1932 and 1939 Cary published five novels, four of which have African settings. Each of the novels deals with a dynamic, innovative, and fundamentally rebellious personality struggling for self-expression and self-realization in an essentially repressive and hostile world. In each novel also the physical setting has a definable impact on the story's development. And in each novel there is at least one African character confronting a modification of the social, moral, and political fabric of his world which threatens to disintegrate his cultural identity. The resulting freedom brings with it in almost equal degree the horrors of alienation and despair, and the opportunities for unparalleled growth and self discovery.

"Daventry"

A precursor of this group of novels, even earlier than the long unpublished *Cock Jarvis,* is the discarded "Daventry." Mahood, who has studied the manuscript of this novel, has written that it is immature, marred by a cynicism characteristic of Joyce in his early years in Africa.[1] Written in 1919, the story recounts the tragic tale of a young colonial officer sent into a hostile pagan area to map and begin building a road. Refusing a police escort, the innocent and gullible young man is led by a treacherous native guide into an ambush in which Daventry and all of his people are either slain outright or fatally wounded by the pagans' poisoned arrows.

Cary based the story on his own experiences as a greenhorn in the Nigerian Service and on an actual event in which an assistant district officer named Maltby was murdered, along with all of his men, when he led them into a pagan area well known for its danger.[2] Reflecting on his dissatisfaction with the story, Cary, according to Mahood, saw the novel's weakness as stemming from "private, subjective elements, prejudices, misunderstandings, and very likely subconscious motives" that blurred what Mahood calls the "universal values which should be the novelist's themes."[3] "Daventry" was set aside as a failed effort and never completed.

Cock Jarvis

The novel presents Jarvis as a willful, arrogant, energetic administrator of a dangerous pagan district which in his former role as a military officer he had conquered. Cary shows Jarvis being plagued, harrassed, criticized, and thwarted by other administrators who resent and deplore his swashbuckling, idiosyncratic, and tyrannical methods of running Daji district. Jarvis, in turn, resents these interferences with what he considers to be his rights as Resident to run his district as he sees fit. In his anger he insults his superiors, writes impertinent letters to the Treasury Department, and quarrels with everyone whom he encounters.

But Jarvis's anger is excessive. So deeply founded is it in his character that the events of the novel serve more as occasion for the release of that anger than the causes of it. For example, at a dinner party Lieutenant Beer, one of the young officers present, maliciously inquires if Jarvis has heard recently from Mr. Bloxam, a colonial officer detested by Jarvis. Although he is aware that the question is intended to draw him into a characteristic denunciation and resenting it, Jarvis stares hard at young Beer and asks himself, "Shall I give him a shock. Shall I tell him what I think of him. If he grins at me then, I can knock his face into his back hair with this bottle. That wouldn't do him any good because he's a smart young man, but it would be highly satisfactory to me" (CJ, 84).

On a later occasion, when he finds his estranged wife with Thompson, one of his junior officers, with whom she had been in love before her marriage, Jarvis is in a similarly ambivalent and excited state. He first tells himself that he will cut out Thompson's heart and choke her with it. Then, following an abortive interview with the two, he very nearly loses his reason: "But then he felt such bitterness that he clenched his nails into his palms, his heart pounded, his head throbbed, his whole body ached and quivered with hatred not only for Thompson but everyone who had hurt him, Killick, Bloxam, Packer and the rest, and his rage became every moment more painful and violent. His eyes were darkened, the blood sang in his ears . . ." (CJ, 161).

The roots of this pervasive emotional turmoil seem to antedate all of the action and may account, at least in part, for Cary's failure to bring the novel under control. As with "Daventry," Cock Jarvis is marred by what appear to be "subjective elements," incompletely understood by Cary and, therefore, beyond integration.

In certain other respects the novel has the strengths on which Cary builds the published African novels. He presents vivid and memorable pictures of African life as in the description of Jarvis returning home across a dangerous river while the Emir and a vast gathering of natives watch the spectacle: "Five persons were crossing in the usual and safest manner, in one party holding on a long branch, and two chop boxes supported waist deep on a raft of gourds, were being hauled across the ropes, amid the obscene curses of the headmen and advice from all the unemployed carriers" (*CJ,* 36). The crossing provides Jarvis with an opportunity to impress the Emir and his people. Taking off all his clothes except for his hat, Jarvis crosses the river alone by jumping from submerged stone to submerged stone. One misstep means being swept away by the very powerful current, smashed among the rocks, and drowned. Jarvis crosses easily, winning the respect of the people for his bravery and skill.

Of equal importance to Cary's emergent manner of writing is the narrative drive that Cock Jarvis generates. In seven lines of text Cary completely reorganizes the entire province of Daji and destroys Jarvis in doing it. Only a few lines earlier Jarvis is shown flying up "the rough path, scrambling over the stones, jumping over holes, hopping from side to side among the roots," and muttering, "Yes, I shall have to shoot somebody." It is no wonder that Cary's writing acquired the reputation of being headlong in its pace.

Ultimately, the problem with *Cock Jarvis* is that it lacks a theme, because Cary does not take a moral point of view in the story. He does not take sides, equally accepting all actions. If Jarvis is betrayed by his friend Thompson, then he deserves to be. If his wife leaves him, she has every right to do so. And thus it goes throughout the novel all the way to his death, an event which is likely to prompt from the reader the observation that while it is too bad Jarvis had to die, it is, perhaps, for the best.

On the other hand, the weakness is also a strength. Freed from the compulsion to pass judgment on his characters and their actions, Cary was able to give full rein to the immense fecundity of his imagination. Events, situations, characters tumble after one another through the pages of his books in a great rushing stream. The result is something disturbingly like life being lived at an accelerated rate. Aside from the comic effects thus generated, there is the sense of some great creative power being released. It is this effect that is one of Cary's foremost achievements as a novelist. His

novels have dazzling vibrance and shimmer. Like Cock Jarvis, they leap
with life.

The issue of religion, which plays an important role in *Aissa Saved* and
The African Witch and a lesser but still significant role in *An American
Visitor* and *Mister Johnson,* is missing from *Cock Jarvis.* Jarvis occasionally
mentions Jesus as a refuge or reference point, and Cary, in his notes to the
novel, mentions the possibility of having Jarvis experience a dramatic
religious conversion. But there is nothing in the novel to indicate those
deep conflicts which arise in the African world from the confrontations of
Islam, Christianity, and the indigenous paganism and which are basic to
the published African novels.

Aissa Saved

Aissa Saved shifts attention away from the white man in Africa to the
African enmeshed in the changes the white man has brought to tribal
culture. In particular Cary is concerned with the impact of the Christian
missionaries on the lives of black Africans. In *Aissa Saved* the Carrs
represent the Christians as the Dobsons do in *An American Visitor* and the
Fortts in *The African Witch.* In the latter, however, the white missionaries are of less interest than the black half-Christian preacher Coker,
whose mixture of Bible pounding and blood *ju-ju* contributes so much
drama to the book.

Although Aissa passes through the triple martyrdom of losing her
husband, sacrificing her beloved baby, and finally being eaten alive by
ants, she dies with a beatific vision of God blotting out all of her
suffering. Much of the dramatic tension in the novel comes from the
conflict between her desire to give herself to Jesus and her equally
powerful desire to give herself to her lover, Gajere. Because she conceives
the "giving" to be a total commitment, sexual as well as spiritual, she is
psychologically incapable of loving Jesus and sleeping with Gajere at the
same time.

Aissa is a "half-bred Fulani girl with big soft eyes and a fine golden
skin very attractive to any man . . ." (*AS,* 14). She is Mrs. Carr's maid
and a recent convert to Christianity. She is also a star pupil at the mission
and a leader of the mission women. She intellectualizes nothing and
experiences everything. It is Aissa's emotional receptivity and clarity of
feeling that direct her action.

Cary is at pains in the novel to show not only the impact a literal and
visceral response to Christianity may have on spiritually vulnerable

people like Aissa, but also how civil strife may be generated by its introduction into African culture. In *Aissa Saved,* as in *Cock Jarvis* and the following novels, there is frequent violence. Aissa is physically injured and mutilated six times in the novel. On the first occasion she is cut in the shoulder by a machete chop intended to decapitate her (*AS,* 61). Next she is charged with being a witch and has her ankle broken from the blow of a heavy pestle (*AS,* 87). Several days later she has her foot amputated by her jailer (*AS,* 104). Escaping jail, she crawls back to the mission at Shibi, arriving "stark naked and very thin," her head shaved, her body "blackened by dirt and bruises" (*AS,* 128). Restored to health in the mission, she again confronts the pagans and in a frenzy of religious remorse, prompted by her inability to resist her lust for her lover Gajere and her love for her son Abba, stabs herself in the face with a knife (*AS,* 202). Gajere is then murdered by the pagans. Aissa, in a final surrender to Jesus, allows her child to be sacrificed to bring the rain. The pagans attack the Christians, and in the battle Aissa has her arms and legs broken and is thrown onto an ant's nest to be eaten alive (*AS,* 211). These are only a few of the violent incidents in the novel.

Cary's point in *Aissa Saved* is that the world is unfair. In his prefatory essay he says that "my book arose from an experience of religion and meant to convey it . . . ," the "experience" referring to his own perception of "the fundamental injustice of the world" (*AS,* 217). Aissa's response to this overwhelming unfairness, which destroys her life, is a dedication to God that enables her to die in an exalted state of religious transfiguration. The novel describes the problems in Africa and the conflicting interests of the colonial administration, the missionaries, and the Africans themselves—Christian, pagan, and Moslem—who are menaced by a terrible drought that threatens them with extinction.

Cary offers no solutions to these various problems. Gajere, Abba, Ojo, a devout Christian, and Aissa are all killed. Ali, the Waziri's fourteen-year-old Muslim son, is tortured to death by the Christian women. A number of pagans are slaughtered in the various fights, and neither the Resident, the missionaries, nor the Emir are able to prevent the murders. The reader never learns where Cary's sympathies lie in the story and, as a consequence, the novel is without a moral center.

An American Visitor

An American Visitor, published in 1933, also had its origins in a real person. This time Cary's inspiration was a young American woman, the mother of three children, who told Cary that she believed children should make moral choices alone and unaided. He found this so extraordinary an idea that he incorporated it into the antigovernment, antiauthoritarian, antirule of law biases of Marie Hasluck, the American visitor to Nigeria, whose trip names the novel.

The real issue in *An American Visitor* is what course of action is to be followed in Birri, the Nigerian province in which the action of the story takes place. The Resident, "Monkey" Brewsher, wants the Birri people left as they are—honorable, brave, and naked. So does Marie Hasluck, who marries Brewsher, largely out of sympathy with his ideas. Cottee and Jukes, on the other hand, want Birri opened in order that they may pursue their tin-mining projects. Gore, the assistant district officer, wants above all to avoid trouble. The Dobsons want converts to Christianity and as little to do with the English colonial authorities as possible.

In *An American Visitor* Brewsher, a character conceived along the lines of Cock Jarvis, wants Birri to be allowed to go along as it has always done without the "improvements" that either missionaries or the commercial developers are likely to bring in their wake. He wants the pagan worship of the god Oki to be formalized and expanded to include an ethical element. Brewsher would also like to see the pandemic infection of guinea worm eradicated and farming systematized.[4] He also wishes to see the various Birri villages joined into a nation. Finally, and most particularly, he does not want to see them clothed or turned into clerks and tin miners. Brewsher is Cary's conservative man opposing anything but carefully managed change. By way of contrast Cottee, spokesman for "progress" and Cary's revolutionary man, argues that Marie and Brewsher want Birri to become a museum by refusing to allow it to join the rest of the world.

Cary gives to Cottee the final word on the subject. Following Brewsher's death at the hands of his Birri, he and Jukes have their tin concessions approved in the Birri reserve. Cottee reflects that "even if civilization meant for the Birri a meaner, shallower kind of life, how could any man hope to fight against it when it came with the whole drive of the world behind it . . .?" (*AV,* 234).

Out of context, the quotation has the ring of a pronouncement in favor of Cottee's view of things. Yet the action of the novel does not support such a reading. Cottee and Jukes are spoilers bent on making money at whatever cost in the quality of life others may be obliged to pay. By entering the Birri lands illegally, they provoke the Birri to violence that leads to their killing Brewsher in the mistaken belief that he has betrayed them and allowed their enemies to steal their land. Ironically, the young Birri warriors are incited to violence by Marie's words when she urges them to be their own masters. She also shares responsibility for Brewsher's death because at a critical point in the action, she hides his revolver because she "had a hunch it was safer for him to trust in God" than in his side arm. Compelled to face an armed and furious band of Birri spearmen with only a pair of sewing scissors, he is killed. So in the end the forces of exploitation and idealism join to kill Brewsher and destroy the Birri forever.

Consequently, the story is inconclusive. In the end all of the parts of the novel flow away between the reader's fingers like a handful of water. Nothing remains. Nothing is left to be said. Perhaps Marie, pregnant with Brewsher's child and preparing to leave Africa, offers some kind of justification for what has taken place in the novel. Speaking with intense feeling, she says that she is finally able to see that "if no one was to die or suffer there wouldn't be any love, and if no one was to get killed there wouldn't be any life worth living" (*AV,* 237).

Cottee hears Marie's speech with a quickening heart and a rush of tears. But he quickly recovers from this "fit of poetical fervor" and, looking at her, reflects that to see "this ugly little woman a tragic queen, Monkey Brewsher a hero, it was absurd" (*AV,* 238). So the spell of meaning is broken and no meaning is left. No more meaning, that is, than would be in a tree or lake or five minutes of random action on any city street.

Mahood, who studied the excised portions of *An American Visitor,* reports that the concern of the novel, at least as Cary conceived it, involves Marie's failure to come to terms with a world that is not ruled by love.[5] She passionately wants security and more or less demands it, first from Brewsher and then from God; but she does not get it, and her husband dies because of her faith, or folly, in hiding his gun.

Does the novel sustain the theme stated above? I think not. Marie Hasluck—the name is a statement—may be an idealist and a sentimentalist; but she is not a complete fool, as she would have to be to make the decision she does make. As the armed Birri pour into the mission compound, Marie turns to Doll Dans, the woman missionary, and suggests they should trust in God for deliverance. Doll agrees and Marie hides the revolver, knowing that her husband must go out in a final effort to face them down. That she does this and that Brewsher does not insist on the gun's being returned to him requires from the reader more than a willing suspension of disbelief.

The reader is simply not prepared for such a development and is not inclined to accept it. No doubt Gore is right to say that Brewsher was bound to get himself killed in the end. One is prepared to believe that, if not the way in which it does happen. Brewsher's manner of dying is too clearly an insistence of the author's that his view of Marie be justified by having her cause her husband's death. The problem is that Cary does not take the necessary pains to make Marie's fatal act the inevitable consequence of her developed character. Mahood sees Marie's action as "the Blakean theme of female domination" working itself out in the destruction of Brewsher.[6] Foster, on the other hand, sees it as "a novel about matters involving theoretical speculation from a distance about what ought to be done" in Africa as opposed to a program of action being carried out by men with an actual knowledge of Africa.[7]

Despite the problem of Brewsher's death and the incomplete development of Marie's character, Cary develops certain aspects of the novel with great skill. As Golden Larson has written, the novel provides "irrefutable proof of Cary's intelligent analysis of the cultural revolution of which he was a part as a British administrator in Africa." Cary effectively sets forth in dramatic form the problem of conflicting interests in the unsettled Nigerial colony. His minor characters in particular and the major characters of Cottee and Brewsher are thoroughly convincing.

The African Witch

The African Witch, his third African novel, published in 1936, continues Cary's interest in the anarchistic white female intellectual abroad in Africa. To this preoccupation he adds a beautiful but stupid unmarried English woman, Dryas Honeywood. And for the first time he draws a portrait in Elizabeth Aladai, *ju-ju* queen of Rimi, of a commanding woman of undisputed power. To a certain degree, all of the women are derivative. Judy Coote, the lame Oxford intellectual, comes from the Punch and Judy show by way of the crazy coot clan. Cary could not have done more to express his distaste for her. Dryas Honeywood is an echo of Galsworthy's Irene Forsyte in *The Man of Property*: beautiful and destructive. Elizabeth Aladai is considerably larger than life. One sees in her Kurtz's concubine in *The Heart of Darkness* or the tinsel mystery of the dark woman in the stories of the H. Rider Haggard variety. Elizabeth goes from success to success in the story, asserting her absolute dominance over the men who challenge her power. The humiliation to which she submits Tom, her lover, adds a unique chapter to antifeminist literature.

Cary based the book, a study of three types of women, on an African character he called the Black Prince, a "violent and hysterical" political agitator who became the model for Louis Aladai, an Oxford educated prince of Rimi, in line to inherit the throne. Of his intentions in the novel, Cary wrote, "My book was meant to show certain men and their problems in the tragic background of a continent still little advanced from the Stone Age, and therefore exposed, like no other, to the impact of modern turmoil."[9]

The absence in the essay of any reference to women, who to a very considerable degree are the catalysts of the action, is intriguing. The book is titled *The African Witch,* a reference to Elizabeth Aladai. And yet the book is or was in Cary's mind about the men in the story, particularly Louis Aladai, Elizabeth's brother. At the end of the novel, however, Louis is dead and Elizabeth seems to be the real surviving center of power, beyond the reach of either the white authority that has become her sponsor or the black Emir who fears her.

Judy, Dryas, and Elizabeth meant something important to Cary, perhaps something frightening. Their power in the novel is deeper than politics or the techniques of colonial and native administration, based as it is on an irresistible attraction and an unconquerable fear. Judy controls through winsomeness and intelligence, Dryas through her commanding beauty, and Elizabeth through her *ju-ju*—a metaphor in the novel for Elizabeth's and perhaps all women's ultimate power to compel men's obedience. Elizabeth's power is also capable of causing death when she feels herself threatened. Mahood's Blakean theme seems inadequate to account for such demonic force. But whatever its source in Cary's mind, he chose to avoid discussion of it in any writing he did about the novel.

In this third novel of the African series the women reach the height of their power and influence in men's lives. Aissa, the passionate convert of *Aissa Saved,* is killed. Marie Hasluck of *An American Visitor* causes her husband's death. In *The African Witch* Judy Coote is, at least in part, responsible for Aladai's death, and Dryas Honeywood dies at the hands of religious fanatics. But Elizabeth triumphs over everyone. Her women's war is effective. She murders the Emir's chief servant after he has tried to kill her. She even manages to win a commendation from the colonial commission for her meliorating influence on the women during their uprising.

The violence that marks and mars all of the African novels is present in *The African Witch,* too, but here it is, generally, a direct outgrowth of the action. Some of it, however, seems gratuitous and beyond the demands of the story itself. Osi, a young African beauty, suspected of being a witch, has her legs burned with coals until she becomes a cripple able only to crawl. A ten-year-old boy is locked in Elizabeth's *ju-ju* house prison and compelled to die of thirst. There is a bloody fight, or beating, in which Rackham pounds Aladai's face into a pulp and knocks him into the river for having had the temerity to establish a friendship with Dryas (*AW,* 202–3). The narrator tells the reader, just as Rackham precipitates the unequal fight, that "the Englishman was a good lightweight. He would probably have taken a Cambridge Blue in 1917, if the war had not carried him straight from school to a training camp" (*AW,* 202). This intrusion by the narrator emphasizes his objective removal from the action. However, it leaves the impression that the narrator either utterly fails to see the barbarity of Rackham's behavior or condones it.

The religious theme in *The African Witch* is most clearly pointed in the blood-madness of Coker, the African evangelist who preaches blood sacrifice and a kind of Africa for Africans. He carries around a human head as his *ju-ju* and feeds his converts to an enormous crocodile that haunts the river close to where Coker holds his mass midnight meetings.

In the prefatory essay, referring to the power of the African material, Cary remarks that when he began *Castle Corner* he wished "above all, to avoid the African setting which, just because it is dramatic, demands a certain kind of story, a certain violence and coarseness of detail, almost a fabulous treatment, to keep it in its place" (*AW,* 311). Africa is vividly present in *The African Witch.* It continuously thrusts its way into the story. The reader finds it in the picture of the old African woman carrying water in a kerosene tin, trailed by a chattering child who calls her Granny; and in the character of the old Emir of Rimi, who was a great warrior in his youth but in his last days prowls the vast compounds of his palace, talking to himself and worrying about a mud wall that has not been repaired. The novel is rich in vivid touches, all of which attest to Cary's power of evocation.

Mister Johnson

In 1939 Cary published *Mister Johnson,* the masterpiece of his African novels and one of the great pieces of twentieth-century English fiction. The story is told in the present, a choice of tense deplored by many of

Cary's otherwise sympathetic critics, in order, as Cary put it, to compel the reader "to swim as all of us swim, with more or less courage and skill, for our lives" (*MJ*, 261).

In *Castle Corner,* which Cary had written immediately before *Mister Johnson,* the narrator says of one of his characters that he, "like other people, created an ideal world for himself but unluckily he did not build facts into the structure." This description of Padsy Foy is at once a description of the man's psychology and an explanation of his actions. Padsy Foy behaves as he does because of the way in which he looks at his world. So does Mr. Johnson in *Mister Johnson.* First and last, what Johnson is, what he does, and the fate which overtakes him are the result of his having created an ideal world from which he excludes essential facts.

The youthful Johnson is a mission-educated Nigerian from the coast who has taken a job of clerk in the remote inland station where the Englishman Rudbeck has been appointed chief civilian officer. Johnson is an ineffective and, perhaps, dishonest clerk, in trouble with the authorities even before Rudbeck takes up his duties. Rudbeck brings to his job little in the way of talent, but he is obsessed with the idea of building roads. It is through the road building project that Rudbeck and Johnson are fatefully joined in the novel's action. As the story advances, Johnson lives more and more dangerously until he commits a murder that results in his own death. The working out of his destiny and the involvement of Rudbeck in it are the central concern of the novel.

Critics have argued that Johnson's dilemma results from the moral vacuum within which he is compelled to live, a vacuum resulting from the disintegration of traditional indigenous values and the devolution of tribal life. Undoubtedly, the Nigeria that Cary describes was undergoing revolutionary changes as a result of the British colonial system, and the elements of these changes are present in the novel. Johnson's move from his own tribal district and the sudden increase in trade between the coast and the interior are two examples. It is a mistake, however, to overemphasize social issues in Cary's superb story. "Africa is too much for everyone in the novel to grasp or control," Robert Bloom has written, thereby presenting the novel as a study of the vast social, political, and economic forces shaking West Africa in the 1920s.[10]

Bloom's observations have a sound basis in history, but Johnson dies, not so much because he is the victim of immense forces beyond his control but because he ignores simple facts which are available to him but which he declines to notice. For example, Johnson shuts his mind to the danger involved in stealing money from the store. He marries a village girl in defiance of his friend Benjamin's warning that Bamu and her family are "ignorant people" who "don't understand anything at all" (*MJ*, 34). Because the facts interfere with Johnson's perception of the ideal life, he rejects them, sometimes with comic and finally with fatal consequences.

It diminishes Johnson to explain him in terms of great forces that sweep him to his death. Such an approach robs him of the grandeur of his folly and the beauty of his delight. He is one of life's great celebrants. He has the gift of continually renewed joy in his world. Taking Mrs. Rudbeck on her first explorations of the region, he repeats a visit to the local pot and basket maker. Mrs. Rudbeck is bored. " 'It's a fish trap, isn't it?' " she inquires, much to Johnson's dismay. He has seen pot making all his life, but he is always interested to hear the life history of each pot, to criticize its form, to argue with the potter about its quality, or to discuss the general state of the pot trade at that moment. To him Africa is, simply, perpetual experience, exciting, amusing, alarming, or delightful, which he soaks into himself through all his five senses at once, and produces again in the form of reflections, comments, songs, jokes, "all in the pure Johnsonian form" (*MJ*, 97).

In this passage the reader has the real Johnson, the man of feeling and exuberance, the man of imagination. Johnson's problem is that he does not have a world to match his vision, and he cannot bring himself to match his vision to the world. In speaking of his wife to be, he says, "that Bamu, she 'gree for me, she love me too much," when, in fact, Bamu feels no love at all for Johnson, merely tolerates him and ignores him as much as possible (*MJ*, 24). Most of the time she even refuses to understand what he is saying to her and despises his manners. Whenever she becomes too irritated with him or whenever he fails in meeting an installment of the bride price being paid to her brother, she coolly packs up her gear and goes home. She absolutely refuses to learn new ways of eating, dressing, or living.

Johnson's marriage adds a comic dimension to the novel and is paralleled by District Officer Rudbeck's marriage, which is also intended as a source of comedy. Cary's presentation of women in the African novels is superb, but his conception of them is often absurd. Celia Rudbeck and Bamu Johnson are real, solidly presented characters. Unfortunately Cary's conception of them is trivial in the extreme. The reader is never allowed to observe their processes of thought and is, therefore, expected to accept their actions as something inevitable. Bamu, although clearly a woman of energy, decision, and initiative, is forced into the role of a stupid, intellectually stunted arch conservative, while Celia, whose marriage is described as "a rocket explosion out of the nursery into the inane," can find nothing "sincere in herself except her nerves" (*MJ,* 107). Both women are compelled to conform to silly, unflattering stereotypes, more removed from reality than even Elizabeth, the Blakean destroyer-woman in *The African Witch.*

The third major human relationship in the novel is the one between Johnson and Rudbeck. Johnson begins as Rudbeck's clerk, is fired, and then rehired as a headman of Rudbeck's road-building crew, a position in which Johnson comes closest to finding a world to match his dream of it. When the road building ends, Johnson is thrown out of work and resorts to stealing money from Gollup's store in order to go on giving gin and drum parties and to continue his position as an important man. One night Gollup catches Johnson in the store and is about to shoot him when Johnson stabs him with a knife and kills him. Rudbeck tries Johnson and finds him guilty, then sentences him to death but recommends leniency on "the grounds of the prisoner's youth and nervous instability." Rudbeck's request for leniency is denied by his superiors, who tells Rudbeck to carry out his sentence and hang Johnson.

What happens in the novel's remaining pages is at the same time both clear and utterly mystifying. It is not difficult to say what happens. While waiting to be hanged, Johnson asks Rudbeck not to hang him but to shoot him instead. At first Rudbeck declines to do such an unorthodox thing and then suddenly appears with a rifle and shoots Johnson in the back of the head while he is on his knees praying. His wife is shocked and horrified by what he has done, but Rudbeck's response is to say, "I couldn't let anyone else do it, could I?"

The action, then, is simple enough, but what it signifies is far from clear. For example, when Rudbeck weighs Johnson in order to decide what length of rope to employ so that the drop will break the young man's neck, he uses as counter balance in the scales bags of money, flour and jam, a choice of articles that reverberates with implications (*MJ,* 240). But the novel does not really sustain the perhaps obvious interpretation that Johnson's life is forfeited for money and trade goods. In fact, it comes closer to saying that Johnson is the victim of a legal system that is completely out of touch with the realities of African life.

But even this argument is weakened by the fact that it is actually Rudbeck who decides what charge to bring against his former head man. Rudbeck is free to try Johnson on the charge of unintentional homicide. Instead he chooses the charge of murder which carries with it a statutory punishment of death by hanging. The responsibility for Johnson's sentence lies with Rudbeck and not with the law by which he is tried. The official account entered into the record is Rudbeck's invention, although as a fabrication it is a good one because it is an approximate description of the events that led to Gollup's death (*MJ*, 236–37).

Rudbeck is, understandably, upset by the prospect of having to hang Johnson. When the time comes to do it, he finds himself unequal to the task. Realizing that he is to be hanged, Johnson sends for Rudbeck and says to him, "Only I tink you do it youself, sah. I don't think you let Sargy do it. . . . Oh, sah, you my good frien'—my father and my mother—I pray you do it—I tink perhaps you shoot me" (*MJ*, 241). Of course, that is at last what Rudbeck does, bringing to an end the most important human relationship in the novel.

The nature of this relationship has been explained in absurdly contradictory ways. Arnold Kettle provoked hostile denials from Cary's defenders by writing that "Rudbeck shoots Johnson as he would shoot a suffering dog toward whom he feels a special responsibility and although the horror of this act is conveyed it is somewhat blunted by the underlying paternalism of Joyce Cary's own attitude."[11] Robert Bloom argues that "the clerk's heroic kindliness and selflessness have drawn Rudbeck, willy-nilly, into a genuine moral and emotional relationship. The recognition breaks in upon his inert consciousness in a way that must leave it forever altered."[12] And Andrew Wright cheers himself by pushing aside the tragic conclusion of the book and writing that "The young African's intense and endless imagining, his creation of a glorious destiny, require that we rejoice in his triumph while we lament his defeat."[13]

There is no indication that Cary regards Johnson's situation as morally wrong or that he repudiates the political and social mechanisms that propel one man into such a humiliating relationship with another. The moral omission is a very marked weakness in the novel. Kettle appears to be right in seeing Rudbeck's feeling for Johnson as one which a kind man might have toward a faithful dog that has to be put down. What Bloom sees as Rudbeck's moral awakening—when he says to Celia, "I couldn't let anyone else do it, could I?"—is light years from a spiritual enlightenment. Rudbeck has, without apparent awareness of what he is doing, made Johnson's expressed wish to die by Rudbeck's hand his own solution.

There is almost nothing in the text to help the reader in his search for an explanation of why Rudbeck shoots Johnson, and the reader is simply not allowed to observe how Rudbeck arrives at his decision. The reader is asked to accept, without observing the process of thought linking idea with action, the proposition that Rudbeck has come to believe that shooting Johnson is his own idea.

If Cary is also asking the reader to believe that Rudbeck's shooting Johnson is an expression of "fellow feeling, a sense of genuine human responsibility," as Bloom suggests, then Cary's failure to understand the horror he has created is complete.[14] But the novel fails to provide any more support for Bloom's reading than for Kettle's. Cary thoroughly absents himself from the conclusion of the novel, leaving his readers to struggle with it alone. It is possible that Johnson's endless improvisations have penetrated Rudbeck's armored soul, finally enabling him to act in a "creative" way, but it is unlikely.

Both Celia and Rudbeck are marvelously insensitive and self-centered. Celia refers to Johnson with the patronizing form, "dear Wog" or "poor Wog," while Rudbeck is simply unaware that Johnson is a human being and cannot even remember to give the necessary orders to have the roof of Johnson's hut repaired. Cary quite specifically says that Rudbeck and his wife "don't notice him any more than a faithful hound" (*MJ*, 167).

Yet, despite the problems created by the novel's ending, *Mister Johnson* is a compelling and at times breathtaking achievement. Page after page of the novel dances with life and energy. The interior of the novel is a fully conceived world, at once convincing and beguiling. Kettle calls it a sustained lyric and, indeed, at its best the story sings. Its chief singer is, of course, Johnson. Johnson's gin parties, his courting, his dancing, and his improvisations are delightful, and it is a dour reader indeed who cannot be brought to smile by Clerk Johnson.

But it is Johnson's work on the road that provokes Cary's most inspired writing in the novel. As headman of all the work gangs, Johnson sets about the task of encouraging his men to greater and greater efforts. He begins by hiring drummers, increasing the free beer, buying himself a folding camp chair with a canopy, and outfitting himself with a white topee. Then he hires a village boy to carry the chair and the hat. At the head of the road where the road is eating away at the towering forest, Johnson sets the drums thundering. Walking among the sweating workers, he takes up an ax or a hoe and pretends to strike the trees and vines, improvising verses for the work songs as he goes. "Bow down you king of cotton trees," he cries and the workers pick up the tune, "Put your green heads in the dust; / Salute the road men of Rudbeck" (*MJ*, 163). The men sing, the drums roar, and the trees come crashing down. The scene is sparkling with life.

The pace of the novel never flags. The reader is borne along on the rush of Johnson's passionate engagement with his work. Johnson loves the drums and the singing. When he stops to encourage a work gang, the chair is set up and his hat placed on its canopy "like a royal crown above the chair of state" (*MJ*, 163). But Johnson never stops long enough to rest. The chair is simply his symbol of office.

Later when Johnson has been warned that he will be put in prison, he repudiates the warning: "No prison," he cries, "take away dat prison. I no fit to go in dar." Indeed, he is not. Johnson belongs among his drummers, urging his gangs of road builders to greater and greater effort.

The African novels constitute Cary's apprenticeship as a publishing novelist. Certain qualities emerge in his writing in these stories which will characterize all of his later work, for better and for worse. Vivid evocation of scenes and character, richness of invention, and copiousness of action are the strongest of his positive achievements in these novels. His work always gives the impression of life closely observed and honestly portrayed.

On the negative side is his tendency to reduce his people, particularly the women, to stereotypes and abstractions. Of greater significance is his drawing back from the action of his novels and failing to provide a moral universe within which the actions may take place. The result of this withdrawal is that Cary's novels do not achieve meaning in the same way that the novels of Hardy and Eliot, for example, do. For this reason Cary's novels stand outside of that long tradition of English literature from William Langland to Iris Murdoch in which the shape of the fictional universe is dictated by its moral center. Cary's art lacks such a center, and at the close of his African period this absence of moral structure remains the most distinguishing feature of his art.

Chapter Four
The Novels of Childhood

Three novels lie between the African stories and the first trilogy, that superb work which marks Cary's maturity as a writer of fiction. The three are *Castle Corner* (1938), *Charley is My Darling* (1940), and *A House of Children* (1941). Written in a four-year period, they are the product of a single stage in Cary's development. All deal extensively with children.

Castle Corner is a fundamentally different kind of novel from *Charley is My Darling* and *A House of Children*. It is essentially a historical novel, a chronicle of Anglo-Irish life that was originally intended to continue for one or two more volumes. Its aim is far more grand than either *Charley is My Darling* or *A House of Children,* both of which concentrate on childhood. Because it is a chronicle, *Castle Corner* will be discussed in a later section.

Mister Johnson appears between *Castle Corner* and the two later novels, marking the appearance of a theme which Cary carried forward into *Charley is My Darling* and *A House of Children*. Wright suggests that from *Mister Johnson* onward Cary's heroes are, simultaneously, creators and rakehells and that these artists ruin themselves for their art.[1] According to Wright the difference between Clerk Johnson and Charley is "hardly more than" one of pigmentation.[2] Although an exaggerated comparison, it does emphasize the close relationship between *Mister Johnson* and *Charley is My Darling*.

The connection between *A House of Children* and *Mister Johnson* is less obvious but still real. Evelyn Corner, the central figure in the novel, is less creative than either Johnson or Brown, and certainly less destructive; but he too is a stranger in an alien world, the world of adult life, from which he is excluded by age and immaturity but toward which he finds himself irreversibly propelled. Larson calls this attraction "the fall into freedom and moral responsibility."[3] The description is interesting but introduces a moral dimension into the three heroes' experiences of which they themselves are unaware.

Childhood for Cary has something in common with interior Nigeria. Foster writes that Cary saw similarities between schoolboys, delinquents, and tribal members, each group having its leaders, pecking order, codes, and taboos.[4] Cary regarded childhood, like tribal life in Nigeria, as a lost world. His method of recovering it is one of the subjects of this chapter.

Cary had a very special and highly schematized sense of what childhood is about. Charley Brown and Evelyn Corner occupy worlds characterized by feelings and impressions. One of Evelyn's earliest and most vivid memories is that of seeing a whale close to the shore where he was bathing. His father pointed out to him the whale's spout and Evelyn says, "I felt the magnificence of sharing bathing places with a whale."[5] He also remembers physical details of the scene and certain things his father said, but it is the feeling that gives the memory meaning.

It is this same centrality of feeling that motivates much of the action in *Charley is My Darling.* Charley Brown, engaged in his first theft, looks at the money he has stolen and then at his companions gathered around him. "He feels the awe and the shock of his followers like something beyond admiration, and he is full of gratitude and affection towards them."[6] Charley is locked into a world of sensation, from which thought is generally excluded. If Charley can be said to think at all, his thinking is merely a process of transplanting feeling into action. After having been arrested and compelled by Lena Allchin to experience remorse for what he has done, Charley threatens to burn the remand house where he is being held (*CD,* 330).

Charley's world and, to a lesser degree, Evelyn's world as well, are chaotic places where event follows event in a reflection of the wildly disorganized mental state of the children. At the same time, there is a fatality at work in the novel; it is the inevitable collision between the child's world and the adult world. As Evelyn Corner says, "Children live in their own world from which all grownups are excluded by the nature of the case" (*HC,* 201).

Cary wrote so frequently about children that he invites comparison with other novelists who have explored the child's world in their writing. One thinks at once of Dickens and such memorable characters as Pip and Oliver Twist and Tiny Tim and the rest. Of course, the moment the comparison is made, the reader can see at once how Cary differs from his great predecessor. Dickens's fictional children wring the heart with pathos, while Cary allows his children to touch the reader only slightly in that way. For Cary the multitudinous elements of life divide into those beginning and those ending. His children, therefore, occupy a world of change. To survive, they are fitted out with the basic Cary survival kit, consisting of strong feelings, the need to give and to find love, curiosity, courage, and creativity.

Charley Brown makes very much the same comment on life as the earlier Clerk Johnson and the later Gulley Jimson. Life is hideously unfair, but it does offer wonderful opportunities for the most exciting experimentation. Johnson is shot to death, Charley is sent to prison, and Gulley suffers a paralytic stroke. Such misfortunes in Cary's world are the result, the inevitable consequence of being free. The same freedom that allows Charley and Liz to fall in love tears them apart. The glory of Johnson's road leads to his death. A bulldozer knocks down the wall on which Gulley has placed his greatest painting.

Of the assorted agonies that visit Cary's protagonists, the most frightening is loneliness. This loneliness is ultimately of a profound order. The condition is absolute and unresponsive to mediation. Cary's sense of unredeemable isolation of the self makes him one with other modern writers such as Sartre and Beckett, to name only two.

Although conscious of man's solitary state, Cary never makes it the center of his fiction. Still, *Charley is My Darling* relies on it for much of Charley's original motivation. Scene after scene in the novel shows Charley alone and painfully isolated. After having his head shaved and his clothes burned because he is infested with lice, he is fitted out with a set of hand-me-down clothes that accentuate his aloneness: "He comes out transformed, the bald skull, the green jersey which is too tight, and a pair of wide, cut-down trousers completely alter his appearance" (*CD*, 15).

The effect of this scene and others like it in both childhood novels is to emphasize the real separation of each individual. This isolation is the real state of things as they are. Charley's brown suit and full head of hair and Evelyn's close association with the other children in his extended family only mask the ultimate loneliness of each child. When the six-year-old Evelyn stumbles along the lane in Dunville village, lost and alone, weeping, he depicts the final human condition.

The two novels link this isolated state with the violence of his youthful characters. Cary's expressed view is that children are violent because "every ordinary child is a delinquent."[7] This assertion comes out of his conviction that until children have "certainties," they will commit crimes as "moral experiments" to see what will happen. Such crimes will, in Cary's view of the matter, leave the child "confused and frustrated, still unable to know, once and for all, what is right and wrong. . . ." He concludes that once in that frame of mind, the child is likely to commit more serious crimes in retribution against a world that "obstinately closes itself to his imagination."[8]

According to Cary, the violent actions in children begin in a desire to understand, and they become engrained when the violence does not produce understanding. The destructive cycle can be stopped only if parents intervene to provide the child with an unimpeded and unambiguous picture of the moral structure of his world. Once in possession of such a picture, a child ceases to be delinquent and no longer finds it necessary to experiment with acts that are destructive or cause pain.

Cary's is a social theory of evil. He assumes that evil springs from modifiable conditions in the child's external world such as boredom, confusion, and lack of understanding. Only two of his characters seem thoroughly, intrinsically bad. One is Adjali in *Mister Johnson,* whose malice remains unexplained. The second is Morton in *Charley is My Darling,* whose viciousness is interpreted as a consequence of his deformity and his mother's having spoiled him. It can be said that Cary has no vision of individual, personal evil. He understands that some acts are antisocial; but there is nothing in his world that is fundamentally vicious.

Charley is My Darling

World War II had been in progress more than a year when *Charley is My Darling* was published. Cary was living in Oxford and serving as head air raid warden at Rhodes House Air Raid Protection Station. The university was in his charge and crucial work on the development of radar under Sir Henry Tizard was going forward there.[9] These details of Cary's personal life did not directly influence the novel, but they exist as very important elements in its background.

Charley is My Darling is Cary's first novel to be set wholly in England and to have a "topical interest."[10] Charley Brown is a war casualty. Sent out from London to the country village of Burlswood, he is found to have body lice and must submit to the indignity of having his head shaved and his clothes burned. His transformation from a decent looking adolescent boy into a caricature figure destroys his self-esteem and his tentative acceptance by the other children.

Charley takes up life in Burlswood doubly encumbered, first as a stranger and second as a figure of scorn and ridicule. The consequences for Charley and the community are marked. Of an aggressive and enterprising disposition, Charley sets out to establish himself as a leader among the

adolescents in the town. He does so against the handicap of being called
Baldy and Lousy.

Charley's name is no accident. A "proper Charley" in English slang is a
person easily duped, perhaps also a person who has made a fool of himself.
The title of the novel also echoes a comic music hall song. Another and
larger irony is built into the word "darling." Charley is the darling of a
pathetic, half-deaf, mentally retarded girl-child, Lizzy Galor. To Lena
Allchin, the adult who is responsible for him, he is only a kind of pet. Her
failure to control him allows Charley the latitude to get into trouble.

Charley's solution to being odd boy out in Burlswood is to behave in
such an exaggerated way as to compel respect. On his first encounter with
Bill, Ginger, and Harry, Charley accepts the dare to challenge farmer
Wicken's bull. Having waved a grain sack at the animal without effect, he
suggests getting some "booze." Not being able to produce the money to
buy it, he agrees to steal it. The theft places him, temporarily, at the head
of a gang, a position he quickly loses and is driven to recover by even more
desperate means.

Once afoot in the country of crime, Charley advances quickly. He and
Ginger break into Burls House, the local manor, and are caught. Charged,
he is released into Lina Allchin's keeping and taken to The Cedars to live.
At the school he temporarily settles into a routine of study and play that
keeps him out of trouble. But it does not last. Given a shilling by Lina and
allowed to leave The Cedars he becomes embroiled again in the fierce life of
the boys in the Burlswood lanes. After three days of adventures, he
establishes himself as leader of the village gang and plans another break-in
of Burls House: "Charley himself made the arrangements, and it seemed to
him, without particular reflection, that there was no other course open to
him" (*CD*, 226).

A second theme developed in the novel is the human need for love and
its immense power to compel action. Lizzie Galor and Charley become
lovers. Wright says that Lizzie knows "simply and by instinct that to love
and succor Charley Brown is her role in life."[11] Predictably, the simple
Lizzie has become pregnant by the end of the novel and cast off by her
family. Condemned to bear her child in disgrace, Lizzie has nothing to
sustain her other than her love for Charley, which may or may not see her
through the approaching ordeal.

Robert Bloom sees *Charley is My Darling* as a novel of "incommunicability." After the final incident at Burls House, Lina Allchin comes to see
Charley in the remand home where he is being held and upbraids him, not

for his crimes but for having gotten Lizzie pregnant. She demands of Charley that he acknowledge his responsibility for what has happened to Lizzie and show remorse. Charley resists but finally breaks down and weeps (*CD, 3*24). Bloom suggests that Lina insists on Charley's acceptance of guilt because she is unable to grasp the nature of Charley's experience with Lizzie.[12]

The fact is, however, that Lina knows exactly how Charley feels. It is because she knows that she is so upset. "Think of what you have done to her," she cries, "—she will have to be sent away from home . . . and you only think of excusing yourself" (*CD, 34*). Charley has told Lina that "it ain't like that," meaning that when he and Lizzie were making love, there was no question of guilt. It is against this absence of feeling that Lina is reacting. In the context of the novel, her conventional morality is inadequate, but to be fair to her, Charley's "naturalness" in his relations with Lizzie is not, necessarily, a better attitude toward sex but only the absence of moral consideration.

Finally, the novel touches on the subject of leadership and seems to ask why people follow a Charley, or, expanding the question to include the Europe of 1940, why they follow a Hitler or a Mussolini. Foster regards the nature of leadership as an important theme in the novel. He suggests that Cary is pointing out a parallel between Charley leading his gang into crime and Hitler and Mussolini leading their people to war; both actions are the result of the leaders running out of ideas that will feed their followers' imaginations.[13]

Charley leads because he has more energy and drive than any of the other boys. Ginger, who gives the impression of intelligence, is not attracted to power roles. Morton, the bully, knows only violence and collapse when he is bested. Lizzie is scarcely competent and does not really think at all. Charley is the center of energy in the group. His enterprise provides his followers with excitement, meaningful action, and challenge. To a lesser degree, he provides them with material goods in the form of automobile rides, money, and loot. He is a bandit chief.

Charley's final act of brigandage in Burls House is never clearly explained. Prior to the break-in the boys have been identified as the thieves who have been troubling the area. "That gives us away," Charley observes (*CD*, 263). Mort then comes forward with a plan to loot Burls House in hopes of getting enough money to escape to Scotland or Ireland. Charley tells him there is nothing to be found in Burls House now that the occupants are gone but that they might have a party there, "jus for a send-off" to "show the cops we knows ow to make a good finish" (*CD,* 266). They have the party and are caught.

No doubt the novel does, as Foster suggests, show "the utter incapacity of humans to live whole, good, and creative lives without love."[14] Charley has no real parental love. Lizzie does love him, and together they plan for a future, not of crime but of work and domesticity in a little house in America. But Lizzie's love is not enough to keep Charley from leading his gang into criminal action. In the final analysis, neither Foster's comments on the need for love nor Cary's remarks in the prefatory note are adequate to explain what is going on in the novel.

To explain Charley as a person would require the special knowledge of a child psychologist. But Charley as a character is another matter. The reader should be able to find Charley's fate comprehensible in terms of his experience and his fictional personality. But it is not really possible to explain the destruction of Burls House in terms of Charley Brown's character as Cary presents it to the reader. In fact, Charley need not have launched his gang on a life of crime at all. The choice seems to have been Cary's rather than Charley's.

A House of Children

A House of Children appeared in 1941 and won the James Tait Black Memorial Prize as the best British novel of that year. In a 1952 letter to Walter Allen, Cary acknowledged that the book has autobiographical elements.[15] The fact is made obvious by the Irish setting and the house filled with children, so reminiscent of his own childhood.

There is general critical agreement that *A House of Children* was inspired by Proust's *A la Recherche du Temps Perdu* and James Joyce's *A Portrait of The Artist As A Young Man*. The novel opens with a conscious echo of Proust: "The other day in an inland town, I saw through an open window, a branch of fuchsia waving stiffly up and down in the breeze; and at once I felt the breeze salty, and had a picture of a bright curtain flapping inwards and, beyond the curtain, dazzling sunlight on miles of crinkling water" (*HC,* 1).

In case the reader managed to miss the significance of the beginning, Cary wrote in the prefatory note, "This book began in fact, as it begins on the page, with recollections suddenly called up by a fuchsia. . . . I was taken back to Donegal . . . not so much to memories as to the actual sensations of childhood . . ." (*HC,* 5). Cary almost insists on his reader's drawing a comparison between his experience with fuchsia and Proust's more famous encounter with the madeline and his subsequent plunge into involuntary memory.

The Joycean influence is less specific but just as certainly present. Evelyn Corner, the protagonist, is a young artist. Seven years old at the start of the novel, Corner is the young Cary. In the prefatory note Cary says that he gave himself an older brother in the story, dispelling any hesitation a reader might have in identifying Evelyn Corner with Cary. The opening pages of the novel describe broken recollections similar to the fragments at the beginning of *Portrait.* Foster goes so far as to say that Cary's technique of depicting the action through flashes of recollection is "rather similar" to Joyce's use of epiphanies.[16]

In *A House of Children* a number of children gradually make the transition from childish irresponsibility and unconsciousness to moral awareness. The story is told from the point of view of Evelyn Corner as a boy, but the narrator is Evelyn Corner a grown man, looking back on his childhood. As Robert Bloom expresses it, Corner's "retrospective insight constitutes the prevailing medium of the book. . . ."[17]

This retrospective insight means that both narrator and reader are distanced from the actual events of the story. Episodes that involve Evelyn directly, such as his peering under a door at a drunken man chasing two girls, are separated by passages of reminiscence that begin, characteristically, with "We were often in mischief . . . ," or some other formulation that pulls the reader back, developing distance and the possibility of irony.

With what might be taken as a Conradian concern to make the reader reexperience the sensations, the feelings, of childhood, Cary uses Evelyn Corner to create the child's limited but intense experience of his world. The reader shares Evelyn's swimming parties, sailing adventures, rat-hunting expeditions, acts of creativity and vandalism, such as pouring water down a chimney (*HC,* 79). While these events are unrolling, the reader is quietly reassured by the voice of the narrator, reminding him that all of these actions occurred in the past. The effect of this double focus in the novel is to give the reader the strong sense of sharing again some of childhood's common experiences. Also, in *A House of Children* Cary breaks down that barrier between the adult and the child world which is so inflexible in *Charley is My Darling.*

Bloom speaks of Cary's triumph over incommunicability.[18] What occurs in *A House of Children* seems to be just that. Bloom's assertion suggests that connections and understanding between those separated by time, race, or culture is possible if both sides remain sensitive to their common humanity and cultivate sympathy. Certainly in *A House of Children* Cary as narrator bridges the gap between his maturity and the distant world of his childhood. For this reason the novel occupies an anomalous place in Cary's work. Its emphasis on connections runs counter to the emphasis in Cary's other work, in which the disparate elements remain rigidly isolated. *A House of Children* offers a possibility for human rapprochement entirely absent from such books as *Mister Johnson* or the other African novels, as well as the first trilogy and *Charley is My Darling*.

A House of Children touches on many of the subjects present in Cary's early work: the meaning and function of love, the force of human creativity, human isolation, the child as a foreigner, the pain of maturation, and the presence of violence in the world. But it presents a picture of life much milder than that offered earlier. In the novel the bludgeonings of fate are reduced to admonitory taps. No action in the novel is as violent as Aissa's death or Clerk Johnson's execution.

The softening of reality in *A House of Children* is not a consequence of Cary's dealing nostalgically with a cherished past. The Irish scene is not sentimentalized. Cary does not appear to falsify his fictive world for the purpose of casting a spell of imagined happiness over it. Neither, on the other hand, does he allow savagery to make it a place of terror. What limits the violence in *A House of Children* is the love and caring that surrounds Evelyn Corner. Although Evelyn and his young relatives are given a surprising amount of freedom, they are kept from ultimate harm by older children and adults who set limits to their mischief and keep them from drowning themselves. In a limited sense *A House of Children* is set in a prelapsarian, Irish Eden, where minor harms befall the inhabitants and some suffering occurs but death is kept at bay. Even Pegeen, the cheated maid, receives her due when the major dies.

Cary obviously has the development of Evelyn as an artist in mind, both as autobiographical analysis and imitation of James Joyce. Two of the major episodes in the novel involve plays. The Corner children write and produce a play that is a humiliating failure and later attend an adult production of *The Tempest* that, in a nod to Blake, alters Evelyn's life by altering his perception of things. The plays also have a decided effect on Harry's life. He never again writes a play and turns his mind to practical things (*HC,* 201).

The children's play proves to be largely nonsense, although its failure genuinely frightens Harry and depresses Evelyn, who, nevertheless, quickly regains his poise (*HC,* 199). Cary uses the play to dramatize a basic difference between the child's and the adult's perception of the world.

Harry's play is made up of an unconnected series of scenes, originating in Harry's imagination and never fully articulated. It is essentially chaotic. Its language is bombast and its theme nonexistent. All that is valid in the play are those powerful feelings that prompted Harry to compose it in the first place, that initial urge which is the deep well of art. *The Tempest* forms a fitting contrast to Harry's failed effort.

Evelyn emerges from watching *The Tempest* in a state close to exaltation. The narrator recalls that "thousands of musical phrases, of half understood images, had fallen upon my senses enriching them as if by three or four years of seasonal falls, flower, harvest, leaf and snow, so that I felt dizzy with the weight of experience" (*HC,* 261). Evelyn is wakened to the beauty of language and to the richness and variety of human emotion. Evelyn thinks about these things for the first time and takes a step toward the understanding of art and toward maturity.

It is not possible in a summary to give a full sense of the richness of *A House of Children.* Two love stories, thoroughly unlike one another, are related, one involving Delia, the novel's most vivid character. Another child, Anketel, slides toward a mental breakdown and then, remarkably, recovers. The world changes. Evelyn comes to see his father as a loved and admirable anachronism. Life is seen as sad and ephemeral as well as comic.

Perhaps the novel succeeds because Cary's limited, and achievable, aim is to present a picture of his early life and a glimpse of those forces which made him into an artist. In addition, the book is almost totally free of galling characters who spring from his ideas rather than his observation. Only Frances defies belief, acting out the same role of woman as deceiver and destroyer that repeatedly mars Cary's writing. *A House of Children* does not have the great moments of *Mister Johnson,* but as a sustained effort it is one of Cary's finest early works.

Chapter Five
The Chronicles

Castle Corner (1938), *The Moonlight* (1946), and *A Fearful Joy* (1949) constitute a group of stories which move through broad segments of time and, in the case of *Castle Corner,* of geographical space as well. Cary's method is to show the rise of a generation, illustrating his argument that man is caught up in a continuous revolutionary change that is the central fact of existence. In addition to this general purpose, Cary attempts to show the progress of particular kinds of social and political changes through specific periods of time. Set in Ireland, *Castle Corner* shows the expansion of the British Empire from the late 1870s to just before World War I, the emergence of Africa as a source of wealth, and the declining position of the Anglo-Irish landowners in Ireland.

In *Castle Corner* and *The Moonlight,* a house is the focus of the action. Closely associated with particular families and their fortunes, these houses enclose in microcosm all the changes occurring in the outer world. The novel encloses the house and the house encloses the world. In *A Fearful Joy,* the character of Tabitha substitutes for the house, and the reader watches the world change through Tabitha's long and event-filled life.

Of the three, perhaps *Castle Corner* has the most ambitious aim. The novel was originally intended, in Cary's words, to raise the fundamental question, "Is there a final shape of society, to be founded upon the common needs and hopes of humanity?"[1] By Cary's own admission this ambitious question is not answered in the novel, probably is never actually raised. Cary abandoned the plan to write two more volumes of the novel and deliberately turned from the vast canvas of the chronicle "to write about the simplest of characters in a simple background, with the simplest of themes . . ." (*CC,* 8). The novel was, of course, *Mister Johnson,* one of Cary's undeniable triumphs.

Cary sensed that *Castle Corner* had not enabled him to achieve his sought after ends even before the book was published and the reviewers had their say. Their verdict was decisive, and stung by the critics' lack of enthusiasm for what he had done, Cary avoided the chronicle form for the next eight years. He wrote six novels during this time, among them the Sara Monday trilogy, but having finished *The Horse's Mouth,* Cary turned once again to the chronicle and wrote two more novels before abandoning the form for good. His purpose, which remained clear and essentially the same in both novels, was to present a unified vision of change that would at once illuminate the destructive force of change and capture from the devastation those enduring qualities of the human character that make it an eternal and parallel force to change in the flux of history.

The first novel, *Castle Corner,* is the most panoramic. By Andrew Wright's count, it contains ninety-three characters. Covering the period from the 1870s to the eve of World War I, it was based on Cary's own experience with Castle Cary, as he knew it while still a child.[2] The scenes in the novel shift from Ireland to Africa and then to England. The thematic concerns of the novel are equally wide-ranging, taking in such diverse interests as the emergence of Nigeria as an important source of wealth, the political development of Ireland in general and western Ulster in particular, issues of moral responsibility in business, and the nature of motherhood.[3]

Even granting that Cary had a trilogy in mind when he launched this literary dreadnaught, the reader is bound to lose his way in the tangle of characters, plots, and ideas. Still, *Castle Corner* is one of those strange books that, while failing as a whole, is fascinating and absorbing in its parts. There are almost no dull pages in the novel. The narrative is extremely lively and the characters delightful. These qualities in the book make it easier to accept Robert Bloom's conclusion that "to admire Cary is, to some degree at least, to consent to what he is doing in" *Castle Corner* as well as *The Moonlight* and *A Fearful Joy.*

In *The Moonlight* Cary was once again to complain that his aims and accomplishments had been misunderstood, a fact suggesting that the chronicle form was not a happy choice for Cary and that it did not suit his genius. Geographically, the novel is more circumscribed than *Castle Corner*: the action is confined to England in general and to a particular house for the most part. The period of time covered is much the same as in *Castle Corner,* from the 1880s to World War I.

In his prefatory note to the novel Cary states that three women, Rose and Ella Venna and Ella's illegitimate daughter Amanda, are central and "essential" to the novel. But another concern in the novel is the disintegration of the family in the twentieth century.[4] Cary felt that a real decline in the quality of family life and sexual practices had occurred in the thirty-year period covered by the novel.

Cary's strategy in the novel is to present the reader with two elderly sisters in fatal conflict over the marriage plans of the young girl, Amanda. Ella, the older sister, who is dying, wants Amanda to marry a young farmer who loves her. Rose, the younger sister, wants the girl to marry a sixty-year-old man for whom Amanda cares nothing. As this conflict is worked out, Cary employs the device of the flashback to fill in the lives of the two sisters and to show the process of social decay which has accompanied the emergence and decline of their generation. Ella is an extremely fine creation, perhaps the most completely realized woman in all of Cary's work.

The third and last of the chronicles, *A Fearful Joy,* also has a woman at its center. Foster calls it "one of the gayest romps through history ever written."[5] While this praise is probably excessive, the book is a vital, even frenetic, work that succeeds very well in conveying the swift advance of time and change. Critics are divided over the book's achievement. On the whole it has fared better than *The Moonlight,* but it still remains one of Cary's forgotten novels. Like *The Moonlight* before it, *A Fearful Joy* was finally shaped to hold an idea, that "in a world so profoundly creative (as this one), what is not in creation withers away; and nothing, no church, no national idea or emblem, no institution, no political set-up, no human relation, can stay alive to the experience unless it be continually reborn and recreated to the imagination."[6]

The actual character through which Cary chose to present this idea is Tabitha Baskett, who falls in love with the rogue, Dick Bonser. Throughout the novel these two come together and separate, and it is their continual interaction that keeps Tabitha alive to her changing world and able to live with as well as in it. The concept of change, personified as the vulgar, dishonest, selfish, scheming, and violent Richard Bonser, is at least exciting. Perhaps less convincing is Cary's portrayal of Tabitha's life being recharged, like an exhaustible battery, by recurring infusions of energy from the source of creation that is Bonser. The novel is crowded with events, like "a film run too fast," in Andrew Wright's words.[7]

Like the other chronicle novels, *A Fearful Joy* is constantly in danger of flying apart from the effects of its own centripetal dynamics. At worst Tabitha seems to be dragged through the book at a pace more rapid than she can comfortably manage, so that she gives the impression of an actress rushing tardily onto the stage to gasp out her lines while trying to put her clothes in order. The novel gives a wonderful sense of life lived, and Bonser is one of Cary's great achievements, even though he is not the novel's protagonist. As is the case with *Castle Corner* and *The Moonlight,* the reader comes away with a sense of having shared delights remembered. Sadly, the entire structure never really coheres, making the novel difficult to retain, except as odd scenes and characters which stick in the memory. While books such as *Mister Johnson* and *Aissa Saved* live as dramatic wholes, the chronicles fail to achieve such solidity and remain a scattering of brilliant parts.

Castle Corner

In 1938 Cary published *Castle Corner* as the first volume of a projected three-volume saga of the Corner family from 1880 to 1935. No one but Cary seems to have regretted that it was not continued to its full length. Cary wrote that he mourned the loss of his characters in *Castle Corner* and their adventures (*CC,* 8). For him, at least, their lives were absorbing and rich in incident. In fact, he had, by his own testimony, written quantities of scenes for the projected volumes to follow *Castle Corner.* The reason that the critics failed to give Cary the encouragement to continue with his project was probably best expressed by Andrew Wright when he wrote that *Castle Corner* has "no central focus."[8]

The problem is not so much one of theme, which is the process of historical decay of social institutions, as it is one of character. The arresting and powerful old man, John Corner, dies early in the story. His sons, Felix and John Chass, do not take his place as centers of interest, although they play important roles in the story. Benskin, the new man of wealth, might have filled the role, as might James Slatter, the Irish neighbor, whose desire to gain control of *Castle Corner* is a destructive obsession.

For Cary the charge that *Castle Corner* was diverse, unstructured, and lacking in focus was especially frustrating, because for him the true focal point in the book is the destructive force of change; it implacably shatters the beautifully ordered society of *Castle Corner* in western Ulster as well as the equally ordered and, therefore, fragile tribal society of Nigeria on the Mosi River.

Cary did not consider *Castle Corner* a finished book. But it is finished. The major threads of the story are wound up, the issues either resolved or their lines clearly laid out. So little of substance is left over that one suspects Cary of at least subliminal awareness of the finality of this volume. One sees clearly that the Castle cannot resist for very long the political pressure rising in Ireland against its Anglo-Irish owners and the deterioration of their capacity and spirit. The Corners are finished as a power in Ireland. Philip Feenix, the lad who surrenders his dreams to his uncle, is dead. Cock Jarvis is off to Africa to test his fortunes and advance the flags of commerce and empire. Sukey is drunk in her kitchen, and her niece Bridget has secured a favored place as her aunt's slavey and a knowledge of where the old woman has hidden her bottle of gold pieces.

Cary was less open about the sources of *Castle Corner* than he was about the sources of other works. Foster has pointed out the shadowings of "Galsworth's Forsyte or Mazo de la Roche's Jalna chronicles."[9] Wright hints at an indebtedness to Thomas Mann's *Buddenbrooks,* another novel about decline, a connection that Stanley Weintraub develops in a close comparison of the two novels that establishes numerous similarities between the two books.[10]

The novel opens in Castle Corner, located in Western Ulster, the Corner family home since the eighteenth century. The time is 1890. Gathered at the family home are three generations of Corners, their extremes represented by John Corner, the patriarch of the family, and Cleeve Corner, the eleven-year-old grandson of old John, home after a nine-year absence from Ireland.

Cleeve's father, Felix, is John Corner's eldest son, but because he cannot agree with his father on politics, religion, or anything else, he has preferred living abroad to quarreling with his father. Now he has returned home to attempt to raise capital for a trading venture in Nigeria, an area that he predicts will soon be making fortunes for the enterprising few prepared to go in early and take risks. He appeals particularly to John Chass, the younger of old John's sons, to whom John Corner leaves the Castle Corner property on his death because he knows Felix would sell it if he could.

Here is an example of that ongoing confrontation in Cary's work between the conservative man, seeking to preserve a past that is inevitably crumbling around him, and the revolutionary man, who welcomes the future and the changes it will bring, even though it will destroy him in turn as it overtakes him. John Corner wants the old life kept on at the Castle. Felix sees that the life of the Anglo-Irish landlord is over, at least in its conventional form, and seeks to salvage something from the approaching disaster by selling the house while a buyer can still be found.

Cary prepares his readers for this mutability on the first page of the novel. Young Cleeve is standing in the breakfast room which faces out onto the lough and looking out over the water, sparkling in the morning sunshine. From this room the house "seemed to float on the lough, sparkling yellow in the April sunshine; like the yacht of some legendary prince in a sea of Rhine wine. But if one looked out of the west windows into the dark green shadows of the trees and the mountain behind, one seemed to be in a forgotten castle where some sleeping beauty in her country stays might eat hot buttered scones for a thousand years and never hear a sigh except from the chimney" (*CC,* 9).

John Chass is one of Cary's conservative men. He is content to live in the Castle, borrow money, and to resist change by a passive lethargy. He is not like his father who fought change in every form. He hangs onto the Castle, clinging like a limpet, and as long as he can, raises cash on mortgages from the banks and his wealthy Irish neighbor, James Slatter, to give to his brother for his trading ventures in the Mosi Company and to finance dinners and dances and the good life at Castle Corner.

John Charles's wife, Mary, does not have a major role in the action of the story, but she forms the basis of one of the thematic centers in the book, the nature of women. Mary Corner is the nest-builder. Her world is centered on the Castle and the life within it. Relationships are the essence of her vision. The functioning of the house, the welfare of the children in and around it, the condition of their tenants' families occupies her attention, to the exclusion of other things. "Her creed," Cary says, "was love" (*CC,* 78). Kindness and love, the poles of her personality, are no match, however, for the antagonists confronting her.

Her son, Shon, is cared for by one of the maids, Kitty, who loves him excessively and spoils the child as much as she can, to his mother's delight. But Kitty is consumptive, and Mary Corner knows it. Kitty should not be allowed to come into close contact with Shon. Mary knows this, too, but her softheartedness prevents her from sending Kitty away. She allows the girl to go on bathing Shon and caring for him, with the consequence that the child contracts tuberculosis and dies. Kitty herself, refusing to confront the reality of her disease, gradually wears away.

Thus, within Castle Corner life goes on much as it has always done, although by the end of the story the reader understands that, if the house is able to survive, it will be because of the money that comes in from the Mosi Trading Company in which John Chass has invested. But the pressures on the house are social and political as well as financial. These pressures are exerted by the rising expectations of the Irish peasantry and the political unrest of the country.

Chief among the Irish characters is James Slatter, who, lacking sons of his own, claims his brother's son, Philip, for his own. Slatter is wealthy and is determined to own the Castle. He fails in that hope as he does in his dream of having his nephew follow him into business. The boy has an opportunity to go away to school, but James dissuades him. Philip then wants to become a missionary and his uncle again dissuades him. Driven in on himself, the young man begins to drink and is soon an alcoholic. Eventually, he marries one of his cousins, has a child, and commits suicide.

Cary's purpose in drawing such a tragic picture of Philip Slatter's life is not completely clear. His uncle is an obsessed man who cannot free his mind from its fixation with the Corners and his determination to own their house and become what they are, a hope doomed to failure by the success of the Mosi Trading Company. Philip looks out away from the cramped world of his uncle's petty dreams and is ready to accept the challenge of the new life. He is, however, seduced by his uncle's promises to make him a wealthy man if he will only stay at home and become a landlord like himself. In abandoning the role of the revolutionary man for that of the conservative man, he seals his fate. Death becomes his only escape.

The two remaining young men central to the story, Cleeve and Cock Jarvis, are both attuned to the future. Cleeve goes to England while Jarvis, an army man, goes to Nigeria and in defiance of government orders invades and conquers a new section of the country, opening it to trade and the profitable expansion of capital investment. Jarvis refuses to accept the limitations of artificial boundaries, moving continuously and restlessly toward new horizons. He destroys much as he goes, but he brings a new world with him.

The man standing in the novel for those forces poised to capitalize on Jarvis's ventures is Benskin, one of the new millionaires. Benskin is interested in Africa and its treasures of gold and tin. Without connections, he makes his way by means of his wit and his capacity to estimate the future.

As a fitting mate for such a nouveau riche character, Cary introduces Helen Pynsant, herself a "new" woman. She is the complete contrast to Mary Corner. Beautiful, flamboyant, promiscuous, she moves through the novel trailing suitors and hangers-on. Benskin manages at last to compel her to marry him and to bear him a child, but he cannot fix her anywhere. She defeats Benskin's attempt to domesticate her. Nothing can do that. She is simply the modern indifference to family life. She bears not a trace of that nest-building instinct so central to Mary Corner's character.

Also carrying a portion of the Cary message in this immense and straggling novel are a great many black and white walk-on characters, who represent in miniature the themes of the major personalities. The Castle Corner tenants are chiefly represented by the Foys, a tribe of hardy Irish peasants who divide dramatically between those whose only dream in life is to work for the Corners and those who strive to break free to build a life of their own. Kitty Foy can imagine no greater joy than working in the Castle, while Con Foy fights the Corners and eventually goes off to America to make his fortune. Like Benskin he is a revolutionary man, an embodiment of that restlessness of history that will finally topple the Corners from their place of power.

It is difficult to remember when reading the African sections of *Castle Corner* that George Orwell's *Burmese Days* was written only four years earlier. The two writers might have been occupying different worlds of sensibility, if not of time. Cary has none of Orwell's anger or sense of injustice. While dreadful things occur to the black people in some of Cary's work, he has none of Orwell's rage against the European. Perhaps this is due to Cary's expressed feeling that both black and white are only instruments of a fatality that has nothing to do with skin color. Men and women are hardly ever evil in Cary's world; they simply act out roles assigned to them by an inscrutable providence.

On the Mosi, Felix settles into his trader's life and accepts Dinah as his "wash woman," a euphemism for concubine. With his own wife conveniently dead, Felix finds it satisfactory to postpone returning to Ireland and, once having returned, to get back to Africa as soon as possible. At the end of the novel he wonders if Dinah has been faithful and is amused by the thought. "But Dinah had her own faithfulness; she was true to her nature, herself, and her needs, and her nature was as firm and dependable as the ground. A man could rest there, at least" (*CC,* 407).

The central fact about Dinah and the girl Bandy is not that they are Africans or ignorant or exploited or doomed, but their basic nature, that is, their human character. In this they do not differ from Mary Corner or Kitty Foy or Helen Pynsant. In Cary's world the human character, not very varied and generally predictable, is the enduring constant in the chaos of change. And whether one is in Ulster or London or on the Mosi River in Nigeria, this fundamental human character occurs and recurs while houses, tribes, and nations rise to power, decline, and vanish.

Castle Corner is so rich in possibilities and so excellent in its parts that it should have been a better book. But Cary failed to find that unifying principle that would enable him to bring the disparate parts into focus. He would find it in the first trilogy, but those books were still in the future.

The Moonlight

Six novels followed *Castle Corner* and eight years elapsed before Cary tried once again to frame his vision in a chronicle novel. These years were of immense importance to Cary. He completed his first trilogy in this period and evolved a narrative method enabling him to hold together the various strands of his story without sacrificing his characteristic richness of invention.

By Cary's own account he was prompted to write *The Moonlight* because of his anger with Leo Tolstoy's depiction of women in *The Kreutzer Sonata,* which seemed to him "ludicrously wrong-headed about the whole matter of sex." Tolstoy's title is a reference to a Beethoven piano sonata, the Sonata in A Major, Op. 47, composed in 1803. Cary's title also refers to a Beethoven composition, generally called the *Moonlight Sonata,* Sonata in C-Sharp Minor, Op. 27, written in 1801. Both novels take the subject of women as their central theme.

In Tolstoy's story a man who has killed his wife describes the action and what led up to it, blaming the education of women for the manner in which marriages are formed and expressing a revulsion against sexuality. Cary was incensed by Tolstoy's novel and determined to write something to counter it. The resulting *The Moonlight* is basically a story about three women, although a number of other women figure in a minor way in the story. The men in the story play peripheral roles, providing the occasion but not the substance of much of the action.

The novel fails largely because of Cary's determination to present Woman instead of a woman. In order to carry out his scheme of repudiating Tolstoy's interpretation of the female character, Cary spreads the action of the novel across a span of sixty years from 1880 to the eve of World War II. He does this to show how the essential character of women repeats itself from generation to generation, modified only slightly by the cultural changes which alter styles without modifying essences. The novel would have been far more effective if, instead of insisting on telling general truths about womanhood, Cary had concentrated on telling the story of Ella Venn, one of his most compelling, if least known, characters.

Cary's ideas about women are appalling. His reductive assertions that women's dress in the 1920s was a product of female frustration with their lives and made them look like "little girls or pederasts" can hardly be taken seriously. Neither can his expressed conviction that in the female "modesty is a fundamental instinct." In his first version of *The Moonlight* he set out to show that women were the prisoners of their sex, that their real dilemma was the inescapable nature of their role in life. "You were born to deal," he wrote, "generation after generation, with great issues, the primal issues of creation, love and birth, the first education."[11] Such inflation was bound to have a destructive effect on the story.

Cary wrote several chapters of an early version "at speed" and set them aside. Several years later he became interested in a story he had heard concerning an older sister who took over the task of mothering a large family and sacrificed her own chances of marriage to the task. By a painful irony her brothers and sisters grew up fearing and detesting her. Cary recalled the discarded novel, recovered it from the attic, and after reading a few pages of it, set it aside for fear that it would "seduce" him from his new plan. It was his idea to describe in the newly conceived novel "the different sexual ideas of two or three generations in their relation with each other and with the final shape of things, the nature of sex itself, of the woman who serves, the woman who rebels . . ." (*M,* 11).

The novel that was eventually completed opens with Ella Venn, aged seventy-four, living in the same house she has always lived in with her older sister, Rose, now bedridden, and Ella's illegitimate daughter, Amanda. Amanda is thirty-two and unmarried and unaware that Ella is her mother. A young farmer, Harry Dawbarn, is courting Amanda, but his suit is complicated by the fact that his farm is in financial difficulty, that he has a village girl in trouble, and that Amanda is lukewarm to his advances.

Ella, however, is overjoyed that Harry has taken an interest in Amanda and wants them to marry. Rose is not pleased by the match. Knowing that Amanda and Harry cannot marry unless Ella gives them money, which she can expect to have once Rose is dead, Rose changes her will in such a way that Ella will be unable to sell the house or to lay her hands on any principal. Although Ella manages to thwart her sister by deliberately losing the will, Rose's tactics do delay the plans of the young couple at a crucial stage in the progress of their relationship, with the final result that Amanda refuses to marry Dawbarn.

The conflict between Rose and Ella over whom Amanda will marry is only one of a series of struggles dating back to their youth, when their mother died and Rose decided to give up her chances for marriage by taking her mother's place in the family and assuming the task of looking after her younger sisters, Florence, Bessie, and Ella. Bessie is chosen by

Rose's rejected lover, James Groom, as a substitute, and Rose uses her influence to compel Bessie to return to him when Bessie rushes home immediately after the wedding. Rose drives her sister back to a relationship which revolts her, despite Ella's furious efforts to make Bessie follow her own mind.

Later, Ella falls in love with a man younger than herself who is married but separated from his wife. Rose and Bessie employ every device to prevent Ella from pursuing the relationship, but she persists and runs away with Ernest Cranage. Penniless, they live in straightened circumstances while Ernest ekes out a living as a warehouse laborer. Although pregnant, not married, and in difficult circumstances when Rose finally tracks her down, Ella pleads with her not to come between Ernest and herself. "If you spoil my happiness, Rose, I'll never, never forgive you," Ella warns her (*M*, 148).

Rose ignores Ella's warnings and separates her from Ernest and then takes away Ella's child and gives it to a married sister to raise. Against the argument of duty and respectability Ella has no defense other than her feelings. These are, of course, ignored by her domineering sister. Ella is defeated. Her life is taken from her.

In these two confrontations between the sisters, Cary sets up the struggle which will end in Rose's death. In a sense it continues beyond Rose's death, because so profoundly is Ella a victim of her sister's tyranny that even after the death, which she certainly wanted but did not bring about directly, Ella is racked with guilt and cannot believe that she has the right to establish her claim as Amanda's mother. In the end she, too, takes sleeping draughts and dies.

In his prefatory note to the novel, Cary wrote that he was "surprised" to learn that his readers considered Rose to be "'a typical Victorian tyrant' instead of the woman of character and unselfish goodness, who had sacrificed her own happiness to her duty." Cary insists that his readers "read into my book what was not there, but which had been floating about in popular notions for a long time—that any Victorian parent who attempted to bring up children to be (according to contemporary standards) good women, good husbands and citizens was a tyrant." He adds that his readers' false opinions "showed me more immediately than I expected how profound are the roots of that injustice, that cruelty of judgement which poisons every age, and especially our own" (*M*, 5).

Cary's idea of what he had written is far from the mark. Rose Venn is no exemplar of virtue but a self-justifying bully who in the name of conventionality, respectability, and propriety refuses her father's mistress access to her father's house, drives Bessie back into the bed of the despicable Groom, and robs Ella first of her lover and then of her child. Her last act is to prevent Amanda from marrying the man of her choice and to attempt to deprive Ella of the control of the Venn property which is rightly hers following her sister's death.

The result for the novel is the emergence of one of Cary's richest and most fascinating characters, Ella Venn. Ella and, to a lesser extent, Rose are three-dimensional characters, locked in their lifelong struggle, a Laocoon frieze. Rose has an iron will and the cruelty to carry out her depredations without mercy or remorse.

What does downtrodden Ella have to confront this monster of self-righteousness? The will to live, to exist, to assert herself even in the confines of her prison. These acts of rebellion are carried out below the conscious level of her own obedient mind. Quite literally, Ella's right hand does not know what her left is doing. It cannot, or the right would prevent her left from acting, and were that to happen Ella would cease to be a person. She would be only a slave to her sister's will.

To see how subtly Ella deceives herself, one has to look no further than the episode, early in the novel, in which Ella loses Rose's amended will. Rose has learned that Ella intends, on Rose's death, to sell the house and to buy a farm for Amanda and Harry Dawbarn in order that they may get married. Rose opposes the match, wishing Amanda, who is thirty-two, to marry Professor Moss, a sixty-year-old man she considers a socially suitable match for Amanda.

In order to thwart her sister, Rose summons her lawyer and alters her will, placing everything in trust and denying Ella the freedom to act as she chooses. She then tells Ella what she has done and gives the will to Ella, demanding that she read it, "because you will be responsible for it after I die" (*M,* 55). Ella carries the will away to the linen room and places it on the hot tank, where if it is knocked over, it will fall behind the tank and be utterly lost:

"It's not a good place," said Ella. "I should have put it away first. If it was to slip down it couldn't be got out again without taking out the whole tank, or cutting through the floor. It would be simpler to make a new one—yes, that would be the best plan." And Ella, reaching up to the row of stockings suspended above the tank, imagined Rose learning of the loss of her will, and then commanding Robin to make another . . . dropped a stocking, grasped at it and caught her sleeve or bangle upon the envelope, which instantly shot down the back of the tank. (*M,* 57–58).

Of course, Ella intends to lose the will. She is making a characteristic fight against her sister, but the effort fills her with terror and guilt. Later on, after Rose is dead and Ella is carrying on about having killed her, her nieces tell her that she has been made to feel that way by the systematic conditioning to which she has been subjected all of her life. But the idea cannot penetrate the wall of conviction of her own worthlessness, ingratitude, and guilt. She is a hostage to her education.

The conscious part of her mind cannot confront the reality of her rebellion against her hatred of her sister. But the reality is there. As Ella runs away from the room where the will is lost, torn by guilt and terror over what she has done, she suddenly thinks, "Oh, it would be easy to hate Rose for hating poor Geoffrey. But it would be wicked. Yes, even if she ruined both our lives and spoilt a great, a wonderful happiness" (*M,* 58). Geoffrey Tew is a young poet with whom Ella falls in love, but who makes the mistake of offending Rose. He becomes unacceptable as a suitor to Ella. Rose sees to it that Ella loses her chance with him as she will later lose her life with Ernest. Thinking of her sister's acts, which have caused Ella so much suffering, Ella thinks, "My poor Ernest, it wasn't fair—but how strong Rose was. What courage she had—what fearful courage to decide lives. She wasn't even afraid to be unjust. Oh, one must be strong" (*M,* 153).

The greatest strength of *The Moonlight* is the emphasis on character. It is unquestionably the most compelling aspect of the novel. Ella and Rose are great achievements. Unfortunately, Rose dies early in the novel and Ella goes before its end. The result of Rose's death is a weakening of the story but the consequence of Ella's departure is its demise. The story of Amanda is inadequate to make up for the loss. In fact, the entire story which embroils Amanda in the Lawrentian conflict between the man of the soil, the farmer, Harry Dawbarn, and the intellectual, Robin, is unconvincing. Amanda's decision not to marry Harry, although she is carrying his child, is not persuasive. The reader can see Cary in the background fiddling with the strings to make his puppet perform the requisite actions. It is a dreary ending to a novel that ought to have been but is not a compelling work of art.

A Fearful Joy

A Fearful Joy fails for other reasons. The last of Cary's chronicles, *A Fearful Joy* approaches the theme of cultural decline from the angle of business and industry and sets out to do for those activities what *The*

Moonlight was intended to do for the family.[12] In addition, Cary hoped in the novel to lay bare the roots of historical change (*FJ*, 6). For Cary the change is caused by "the whole world seeking escape from boredom." In the desire for escape "the world" finds inspiration in the "spell-binder," who is, as often as not, a crook but who, nevertheless, inspires in his victims the passion for life.

Cary points to the central weakness in the novel when he writes in his prefatory note that "the work was too small for its theme" (*FJ*, 6). This was said about a draft of the novel which he eventually abandoned, but it remains true of the final version, though not in the sense that Cary meant. Cary felt that one volume would not be enough to deal fully with the nature of change and permanence. Eventually, he found a way to tell his story in one volume, but he failed to solve the real problem plaguing the novel, which is that Tabitha is not sufficiently significant a character to carry with conviction the weight of meaning Cary puts on her. Similarly, Bonser, the petty crook and woman beater, is scarcely convincing as the repository for that energizing force that, in Cary's view, keeps mankind from perishing of inanition.

The novel tells the story of Tabitha Baskett's life from birth to a point just short of her death. Like other Cary women, Tabitha is a product of middle-class upbringing in the late 1900s and a rebel against its constraints. Unlike Ella in *The Moonlight,* Tabitha breaks away from her home to follow a young ne'er-do-well, Richard Bonser, who takes her away with him, spends her money, refuses to marry her despite his promises, and punches her in the face and leaves her when he discovers that she is pregnant. From time to time throughout the novel Bonser reappears to work more mischief. But Tabitha is delighted by her rogue, whom she does finally marry, despite the protests of her friends.

Cary's intention is to show that Tabitha's life, inclined toward respectability and dullness, is constantly revivified by the interventions of Bonser, who brings her liveliness and joy. Tabitha repeatedly remarks on the joy which she feels when she has done some new and outrageous thing with Bonser. She knows well enough that Bonser will never settle down or be faithful or make any great effort to look after her, but this is unimportant. He gives her delight. Her life is quite free of delight when Bonser first appears in it, and she is certainly ready for a change.

As a young woman, bored with her life, Tabitha cries out, "Oh—oh—oh, if only something would happen!" (*FJ*, 5). Something does happen, in the form of Richard Bonser. She runs away with him—ignoring warnings from her brother and his wife—and begins that long pilgrimage that will

finally end at the eve of World War I. By the time the novel closes, she has
a grandchild, Nancy, who has chosen her own life with a rotter, just as her
grandmother did. The events between Tabitha's flight from her home and
her decision to help Nancy to make a home are designed to illustrate the
rapid cultural changes that swept across Europe from 1900 to 1940 and
the swift expansion of business and manufacturing brought on by the
making of automobiles and airplanes.

Tabitha has a son, John, who is for a time led into the study of engines
and mechanics when Tabitha marries the industrialist James Gollam. But
John's mother persists in prodding him into a scholarly direction and the
boy goes to Oxford. Later he marries a hard young woman named Kit,
whom he treats very well and who kills him through neglect. Tabitha and
Bonser eventually marry and settle into the hotel business—at least
Tabitha does. Bonser continues on his way much as before, eventually
managing to die in a low class whorehouse. He dies in Tabitha's arms,
gloating that he had "Got away every time—spoofed 'em, spoofed the
whole—" (*FJ*, 39). Death silences him.

The novel is undeniably fast moving and filled with event. The scenes of
London literary life in the first quarter of the book, during which Tabitha
becomes associated with *The Bankside,* a periodical modeled on *The Yellow
Book,* are amusing. In them Tabitha begins to emerge as a complex
character, only to fade again as Cary's interest in showing the sweep of time
washes her out of the center of attention. This happens, at least in part,
because the story moves too swiftly, covering too much ground and
concerning itself with things, such as the manufacture of airplanes and the
management of hotels, which are not germane to the novel's concern.

But there is a quality of the novel which has gone unremarked. Cary is
often praised for his portraits of woman. Noble writes that Tabitha is one
of the best aspects of the book.[13] Foster calls the book "One of the gayest
romps through history ever written."[14] Others speak of Cary's interest in
the perpetual revolution and in feminine worlds. However, in this novel
Cary's portrait of woman is insulting. The undeniable message which
comes out of the pages of *A Fearful Joy* is that women are best treated by
being abused, and that when they are not abused, they become destructive. They are predatory and exploitive, selfish and vindictive when not
hammered into compliance.

In the novel the first hint of Cary's attitude toward women comes when
he describes the process of Harry Basket's marriage. "Like many good,
serious young men who never flirt, he was caught by the first determined
young woman who wanted him, and at twenty-eight was already the slave

of a house" (*FJ*, 2). The wife, Edith, is described as "handsome, sensual, rather blowsy, fond of bright colors and rich food, critical, like a woman much loved, of her husband . . ." (*FJ*, 4). Edith's shortcomings do not stop with self-indulgence and cynical disregard of her husband's sensibilities. She manages to quarrel with Harry's father in order to drive the ailing widower out of his own house and into lodgings, where he dies within six months. Harry allows this to happen by not defying his wife.

Throughout the rest of the novel, Harry's life is made a burden by this wife who bears children carelessly, is a poor housekeeper, allows herself to grow fat and unattractive, and gives her husband a minimum of comfort during their life together. Harry, however, remains a dutiful husband and is abused for it. Tabitha's son, John, is treated in a similar way by his wife. Settled as a university teacher in the ugly provincial city of Urrsley, he encourages his wife to open their house to her friends. A man named Rodwell, who may be his wife's lover, makes fun of John in his own house in front of his friends and is encouraged by Kit to do so. Kit finally insists on John's going rock climbing in Wales, despite the fact that he fears heights. He contracts pneumonia and dies, killed by his wife's refusal to admit that he is seriously ill.

In contrast with the fates of Harry and John, Dick Bonser contrives to die in a whorehouse, a temple of female exploitation, crowing over his success in having managed all his life to escape from the women who would have trapped him and nailed him down to suffer for their delight. Having seduced Tabitha, he runs off with the next woman who catches his fancy, leaving Tabitha in a hotel with no money and an unpaid bill (*FJ*, 15). She goes home to Harry, who, of course, takes her back into his house. But she runs away with Bonser again, who is broke and knows she will bring him some cash. They live together for a while until she becomes pregnant. Then she tells him that "this baby is yours, too, and you've got to do something about it." Bonser responds to this charge with physical violence. "At this moment Tabitha feels in the middle of her face a dull painful shock, and finds herself lying on her back in the midst of darkness . . ." (*FJ*, 38). Bonser has struck her full in the face with his fist. Picking up his bag and his coat, he leaves her a second time.

This time Bonser stays away for several years, but he turns up again, in another attempt to get money from Tabitha. She refuses but feels no resentment. On the contrary, "she is laughing, her eyes sparkle; her cheeks glow; a mysterious energy pours through her nerves." She begins sending him five pounds a month on the basis that "it's worth it to get Dick's nonsense" (*FJ*, 38). Over the ensuing years Tabitha marries, is widowed, and meets Bonser again, finally marrying him and finding herself "full of a secret abounding delight" (*FJ*, 219). Tabitha sells out her war loans, worth several thousand pounds, and gives the money to Dick, who buys a hotel and makes a success of it by turning it into a road house, a place of assignation and accommodation for the fast, motoring crowd. He even moves his current mistress into the hotel as an employee. Tabitha bears it all, and Bonser continues as a bounder all his days. When he dies, though, the local papers write him up as a public benefactor and Tabitha says of him that "he brought me to life again; it was like a resurrection from the dead" (*FJ*, 317). Dick Bonser is justified in Tabitha's final reflections on him. His treatment of her has been terrible, but she thrives under it.

The tale is not finished with Bonser's death. Tabitha's granddaughter, Nancy, falls in love with an air force pilot, Joseph Parkin, and becomes pregnant. She refuses to "blackmail" Parkin into marrying her and Parkin declines to accept responsibility for Nancy's condition. Tabitha offers money and "Joey" agrees to think it over. Reporting to Nancy on her progress with Parkin, Tabitha asks her granddaughter if she and Parkin have any respect for one another. Nancy replies that she does not "know about respect, but I admire Joey, he's a terrific person. He doesn't care for anybody or anything." Tabitha settles three thousand dollars on Nancy, and Parkin agrees to marry her. He marries her in a registry office and does not even stop with her once the ceremony is over. Nancy defends this brutal behavior on the grounds that he " 'hates being made to do things, and he never puts on an act. He's terribly honest' " (*FJ*, 292).

Nancy's life with Parkin after he leaves the air force is a long burden of poverty and children. He treats her less well than he would treat a servant and she worships him for it. Tabitha again comes to the rescue with money and, for thanks, when Parkin decides to move to New Zealand, he makes it clear that he does not want Tabitha with them. Nancy is so grateful to Parkin for asking her to take the children and come with him that she makes no protest at leaving Tabitha behind. They go. Tabitha is abandoned to her loneliness. She has even paid for their air fare and arranged an allowance.

These actions by Bonser and Parkin are supposed to represent the revivifying force of life that bubbles up eternally to fructify the earth and keep the world from stagnating. But Bonser and Parkin are simply not up to their roles. They are selfish wasters who bully and brutalize women and reap an endless harvest of love and affection for their sullen crudities. Their characterization is an outgrowth of Cary's view of women and how they should be treated.

A Fearful Joy brings to an end Cary's efforts to employ the chronicle form in his novels. In one way or another all of them fail because he fails to find a way in which to hold their centers together. Cary's greatest strength is in characterization, and his stories are at their best when the narrative is centered on one or another of his characters. In the chronicles he sacrifices this strength to develop abstract ideas, such as the inevitability of change, or the nature of women, or to emphasize an historical panorama. The technique fails, but the three novels are, nevertheless, memorable ruins.

Chapter Six
The First Trilogy

In one sense, the novels composing Cary's *First Trilogy* can be regarded as another attempt by the novelist to write a chronicle. Having failed in his earlier efforts, Cary scrapped the forms he had been employing and adopted an entirely new approach. He broke up the point of view, distributing it among three characters, each of whom became the protagonist of one of the novels. Sara Monday is the center of interest in *Herself Surprised,* the first novel in the trilogy; Thomas Wilcher, the focus of the second, *To Be A Pilgrim*; and Gulley Jimson dominates the third, *The Horse's Mouth*. The period of time covered by the novels is about seventy years, roughly the time encompassed by the life of Thomas Wilcher.

In this new chronicle each of the characters tells his own story, revealing an "aspect" of the total experience while, at the same time, painting a self-portrait. In his preface to the trilogy, Cary admits that the three books are not "a trilogy at all in the ordinary sense of the word." By this he means that the volumes do not follow one another in strict chronological succession. *To Be A Pilgrim,* for example, the second novel in the sequence, reaches back into an earlier period of time than does *Herself Surprised,* the first book in the trilogy. Cary also means that each volume possesses a distinct style dictated by the personality of their respective protagonist-narrators. Cary writes, "Each of the three characters are to know each other and have some connection in the plot, but they would see completely different aspects of each other's character."

But, of course, the three stories are inextricably linked, although each novel can be read satisfactorily without reference to the others. The full effect of the novels can only be experienced, however, by reading all three of them and, preferably, by reading them in proper succession. Read in this way, the novels reveal the full extent of Cary's success. Beyond any doubt, in *Herself Surprised, To Be A Pilgrim,* and *The Horse's Mouth* Cary has his most impressive triumph as a novelist. Sara Monday, Thomas Wilcher, and Gulley Jimson are intensely realized characters, rich and compelling, and occupying fully articulated worlds.

As so frequently happened with Cary when he began to write, he found that he had to alter his original plans for the books. He intended to have each of the characters tell how he or she felt about art, politics, religion, family life, and life in general. But Cary discovered that his plan had "unexpected flaws." He found that when Sara began to talk about politics and art, "she became less vivid a character. She lost immediacy as a family woman." So, too, and for the same reason of declining vividness of character, he was obliged to delete Wilcher's comments on art in the second volume and Gulley Jimson's on politics in the third.

Cary's comment on this matter is of great importance in showing how he perceived characterization. Cary insists that when he was faced with a choice such as this one, his rule was "character first. . . ." Such a statement might prove confusing to a reader who assumes, understandably, that the richer and more complex a character, the more "vivid" he is likely to be. But that is not Cary's understanding of the situation. For instance, he made Sara more vivid by limiting her scope.

Clearly, for Cary, "character" in the trilogy means something it has ceased to mean in Western literature for more than two hundred years, that is, type or kind. Sara is to be "a family woman," and "vividness" is to be judged in terms of the intensity with which that aspect of her being is developed. In fact, as a character she is to be a family woman and as little of anything else as possible. That is why Cary felt a sense of loss when Sara began to talk politics and art. Her "roundness" as a character is not Cary's aim. She is to be a nest-builder, a home maker, and everything that does not reflect this fact of her being has to be ruthlessly cut away.

Herself Surprised

It is difficult not to wonder how Cary's career as a writer would have fared had he reached the height of his powers during peacetime instead of during a world war that threatened to obliterate the cultural and political life of the Western democracies. Perhaps it must be counted as a minor miracle that Cary and other writers continued to be published at all, even granting that the use of material and manpower used to produce works of fiction was justified on the grounds of maintaining civilian morale.

Although it may sound like black humor, 1941 was what Foster calls a "banner" year for Cary. He published two novels, *A House of Children* and *Herself Surprised,* in addition to the political pamphlet, *The Case for African*

Freedom, which Cary regarded as an important statement of his views regarding the political future of black and white Africa. It had been published earlier as a pamphlet in the Secker & Warburg series, "Searchlight on Africa."[1] Since *A House of Children* won the James Tait Black Memorial Prize, it threw into relative obscurity his second novel of that year, *Herself Surprised,* which, nevertheless, managed to have a modest popular success. By the time *Herself Surprised* had made its way into print, Cary was nearly finished with the second volume of the trilogy, *To Be A Pilgrim,* and was beginning to think about a third volume.[2]

Sara Monday, the protagonist of *Herself Surprised,* is the central figure of the trilogy. Even when she is not on stage in the second and third volumes, her influence is felt through the minds of the two male protagonists. She is a fixed center and one of the principal axes on which the stories turn. Born about 1880, Sara is a country girl, whose mother puts her into service with the idea of making her into a first-class cook, a plan which succeeds. Sara leaves her country village to live in Bradnell Green and cook for Mrs. Monday, a widow, and her adult son and daughter, Mathew and Maggie.

Herself Surprised is Sara's story of her life from these beginnings to her imprisonment for theft. Sara writes her story in prison as a memoir which she has sold to a newspaper for 100 pounds, money she needs to pay Gulley Jimson's bills and to keep their son, Tommy, in school. Even in prison she remains true to her character of nest-builder, finding a way under every circumstance to keep active as a nurturer.

Because her audience will expect contrition, Sara's narrative is laden with pieties and homilies on the price paid by sinners and on her own culpability. Sara never denies that she is guilty as charged in court and even insists that had the truth been fully known, things would have gone much worse with her. As she says, "I couldn't deny that every little bit they brought against me was true; or nearly true; and some things that they did not know were worse."[3] Having taken on the burden of her sins, she explains that she is telling the story in order that "some who read this book may take warning and ask themselves before it is too late what they really are and why they behave as they do" (*HS,* 2).

In spite of what she says, Sara does not feel the slightest genuine guilt for her actions. In fact, during her sentencing, the judge upbraids her for behaving like a woman without any moral sense. "'I noticed . . . that during the gravest revelations of her own frauds and ingratitude, Mrs. Monday smiled. She may be ill educated, as the defense has urged, but she is certainly intelligent. I am forced to conclude that she is another unhappy example of that laxity and contempt for all religious principle and social obligation which threatens to undermine the whole fabric of our civilization" ' (*HS*, 1). Cary's purpose in introducing this passage is to give the lie to Sara's protests of remorse, on the one hand, and to bring before the reader at once the conflict between a rational system of social intercourse as represented by the judge and his body of law and the natural force embodied in the character of Sara Monday, whose living energy has nothing to do with legal abstractions.

The problem of Sara's faith is something else. In response to the judge's charge that she harbors contempt for religious principle, she says, justifiably, that she was brought up in a good home and knew the difference between right and wrong. In *To Be A Pilgram,* when Ann suggests that Sara "rather affected the religious," Thomas Wilcher sharply contradicts her. "No," he responds, "you are quite wrong. She never affected anything, but she is deeply religious. She is one of those people to whom faith is so natural that they don't know how they have it. She has a living faith."[4]

Wilcher's interpretation fits well with Cary's perception of Sara. As a nest builder, a prototypical woman, she is not at all self-aware. The title of her story, *Herself Surprised,* is definitive. Sara is constantly being surprised by her actions, especially those which she calls "evil." The reason she is surprised is that she does not really regard them as evil.

Reviewing her married life with Mathew Monday and the pleasure she took in it, she makes a kind of defense in which she reveals herself:

For in all our happiness there was more religion, and no one in Bradnall, however gay, would have thought of tennis on Sunday, or of not going to church. If I went to the bad at the last, it was not the fault of the times, but of myself. . . . For many were as gay, who were also good, and happiness was a grace to them, as it is God's most precious grace; they lived with God and never forgot their gratitude. So I have thought, even at a ball; this sweet pleasure is provided for me, and felt the wonder of God's providence and my own especial luck. (*HS,* 37)

Although she does say that she forgave herself too easily for her faults, the statement clearly suggests that she felt the special presence of God's grace in her life and counted herself among those enjoying "God's Grace." Her so-called evil acts were principally sexual, although she says, in fine textbook fashion, that they began in vanity and were nurtured by greed. Sara is fat and has always had a sweet tooth. Sara is also an intensely sexual being, whose "surprises" came frequently from early in life to the end. She condemns herself for these lapses from strict monogamy, but takes it back in the next breath by saying God had made her that way. Mathew Monday accuses her of "having no idea of right or wrong," and in his sense of the phrase he is quite right. But it is not Sara's sense.

Perhaps the best representation of Sara's idea of religion occurs at the end of chapter 28 when she and Gulley are sitting late at night in front of the kitchen fire, drinking toasted ale. Her husband, suffering from a serious heart condition, lies asleep upstairs, having taken a sleeping draught. "Believe me," she says, "the kitchen fire is the sweetest fire in the house, for confidence and for lovers, and for consolation, and for religion too, I mean facing the world" (*HS,* 83). Sara reads a lesson on life out of the fire that has the ring of truth to it. For once, she is not being pious by design. She calls it "a useful fire and not just luxury; and it is so made that it drops its coals and tells you, with every fall, that life burns away, and it has the stove top for a kettle to remind you that, at the worst there is always tea, and that the best comforts are at everyone's hand" (*HS,* 83). Sara's "facing the world" is living in it, resigned to its passing and consoled by its comforts. For Sara living is religion.

It is important to be clear concerning Sara's moral status, because Cary makes a point of contrasting the responses to life of each of the three protagonists. Thomas Wilcher is a conserver, Gulley is a creator, and Sara is so deeply immersed in life that she cannot be said to have an intellectual perception of it at all, beyond the essentially sensuous one embodied in the fire. She often observes that she considers religion important. She even talks with Gulley about it. And it is in her book that Gulley makes his most definitive statements about it. But it comes down to nothing more serious in the way of inquiry than her asking how she looks in her new hat. She is secretly pleased when Gulley tells her not to worry about religion, that "it's bad for your figure and your hair." And, again, " 'You're Mrs. Em and I'm Gulley Jimson and that fly on the wall has its own life too—as big as it likes to make it, and it's all one to God, as the leaves to the tree" (*HS,* 83).

In this respect I think Robert Bloom carries his useful concept of indeterminateness in Cary's writing too far. He complains that "we cannot place Sara, with any real assurance, as a moral being"[5] He concludes that it is one of the great comic attractions of the book that we are unable to do so. He reads Sara's "surprises" as counterfeit astonishments, generated for the purpose of excusing her dubious actions, such as committing adultery with Hickson. It also appears that she is occasionally surprised by the garden boy, perhaps even the milk man.

The key to Sara is her way of understanding the world, and she understands it through her feelings. What she does not feel is not real to her. She does not feel that there is anything wrong with stealing in small ways from Wilcher while she is his cook and mistress in order to keep Tommy in school and Gulley supplied with money. As Andrew Wright has written, Sara is unreflective. She never gains enough knowledge of herself to "see into her own heart." She is not being deceptive or self-blinding when she says that she regrets the things she has done "but she does not feel it, and feelings are all in all with Sara."[6] What passes for deception in Sara is, finally, the consequence of a totally subjective being attempting to explain herself to a world that judges right and wrong by standards which to her are impenetrable.

Much more serious than the degree to which Sara is a self-deceiver is the long descent of her fortunes throughout the trilogy. Briefly stated, Sara begins as a good cook, marries considerably above herself, squanders her widow's inheritance over a period of five years with Gulley Jimson, and finally is brought before the magistrates for writing bad checks. While she lives with Gulley, he beats her twice, the second time savagely, and abandons her for another woman. Now without a character, she goes to work for Thomas Wilcher, becomes his mistress, and is eventually arrested and sent to prison for stealing from him. Out of prison she lives with various men, each move taking her further toward brutalization. The last man she lives with, Byles, abuses her, and, at last, Gulley hits her on the head, knocking her downstairs and killing her. Her last act is to give a false description to the police of her attacker, to protect Gulley.

In many ways the closest Sara comes to having the kind of "home" Cary mentions in the prefatory essay to the novel is the time she spends as cook at Tolbrook, Thomas Wilcher's family home. But her good fortune is brought to an end when one of Wilcher's nieces finds out that she has been stealing from Wilcher. She is then imprisoned for two years. Released from prison, she becomes a "housekeeper" for at least two more men while still managing to keep in touch with Gulley. In a desperate attempt to get money, Gulley tries to recover one of his early paintings from Sara. She misleads him, depriving him of the painting. When he discovers the trick, he returns to steal the painting, and when she tries to stop him, he attacks and kills her.

Sara's tragedy is not one of having her children leave home or of growing old, for to the end of her life she remains full of spirit and good temper and readiness to love. Her fate is to be used by men who have very little regard for her needs or wants. A lengthy parade of men welcome her ready sexual response, enjoy her cooking, and, with the exception of Gulley, accept her mothering. But not one of the men treats her as anything other than a convenience. At the end of his life Wilcher tries to marry her, but he is too old and sick for Sara to take his offer seriously. She gives him back into the keeping of his niece Ann, who returns him to Tolbrook, more or less a prisoner. He is treated as a mad old man, but he comes to recognize Sara's worth as a human being and puts himself into a relationship with her that is based on mutual respect, although it can be argued that Wilcher's perception is largely self-deception.

It is difficult to follow Cary's thinking in his plotting of Sara's fate. Why, for instance, must she be struck down and killed by Gulley, the one man in her life she truly loves? Is this death a part of the "tragedy" that Cary outlines in the prefatory note? It certainly does not follow that women who seek to make a home for themselves and their men must die violent deaths. Then what accounts for her murder? The answer lies in the mostly unstated view of women that runs throughout Cary's work. That view holds that women have to be kept down by whatever means one has at one's disposal. The most direct is physical violence. When they are not kept down they become destroyers and tyrants.

So Gulley begins by popping Sara on the nose because she attempts to organize his life along lines of order that seem rational to her but stultifying to Gulley. The blow he strikes is a blow for artistic as well as individual freedom, and he goes on knocking her about until he finally kills her. The close of the novel leaves the reader with the impression that Sara is quite satisfied to have been murdered by her old lover. Not only does she give the police a false description of her attacker, but her ghost warns Jimson as he is working on *The Creation* to get down off his swing before he is hurt. Gulley chaffs her about having taken the whole world to her bosom and she says, "'And you don't really want me?'" His response is, "'Not just now, my dear.'"[7]

Sara's death is completely acceptable in the novel. That she was killed is of little importance to Sara. She goes on attempting to mother Gulley, even pimp for him, from the next world. Gulley says of his murder of Sara, "materiality, that is, Sara, the old female nature, having attempted to button up the prophetic spirit, that is to say, Gulley Jimson, in her placket-hole, got a bonk on the conk, and was reduced to her proper status, as spiritual fodder."

The statement, sounding like a justification for the physical abuse of women, raises a further question. Sara is either a character deserving the reader's sympathy and affection or she is merely a symbol. If she is a symbol only, then what happens to her is unimportant, at least of little interest. If, however, she is a fully realized character, killing her cannot be simply a dramatic representation of a Blakean formula.

Another complexity in Sara's character is a consequence of the echoes which surround her. Foster finds resemblances between Sara and Moll Flanders, the Wife of Bath, Mistress Quickly of Shakespeare's *Henry IV* and *Henry V*, and Sean O'Casey's Juno.[8] One might add Venus, Ceres, and Cybele, to round out the associations. In his efforts to create his version of an archetypal female, Cary inevitably suggests all the other fantasy women of mythic stature whom she resembles.

Foster points out that Cary disliked having Sara compared to Moll Flanders and that Cary denied being influenced by Defoe, even though a letter to his wife suggests that he knew Defoe well.[9]

Perhaps Cary feared that if readers connected Sara and Moll they would regard Sara as a woman of loose morals and thus miss the point he wished to make regarding her drive to create homes for herself and her men. But it seems impossible to escape the fact that Sara is sexually promiscuous and, like Moll, a thief, even if she is also warmhearted, generous, good natured, and a vigorous worker.

It is also possible that Cary was made uncomfortable by the suggestion that he had added another document to the long catalog of antifeminist creations, to which the Wife of Bath and Moll Flanders can be construed to belong. Cary need not necessarily have been motivated by malice toward women in creating an antifeminist portrait in Sara Monday. He would have succeeded in making one had he done nothing more than follow the models provided by Chaucer, Shakespeare, and Defoe. O'Casey is another matter entirely. His character of Juno is nearly free from conventional antifeminist traits, but she does resemble Sara in her desire to marshall all the members of her family into an alliance of work and respectability, dedicated to keeping an orderly, prosperous home. One remembers in this regard Sara's conviction that the only reason Gulley is not making a lot of money is due to bad management on his part, a condition she is eager to remedy.

As Giles Mitchell has written, Sara is one of the constants underlying the apparent chaos of created existence.[10] She is central to the trilogy, and it is impossible to imagine the second and third volumes without her in them. She is a steady point of reference for both Wilcher and Gulley Jimson, one to which they constantly return and from which they go out in their quests for knowledge and artistic expression. She is one of Cary's most successful characters, fully realized and convincingly rooted in the context of the tales.

To Be A Pilgrim

Cary's second novel in the trilogy was published in 1942, a year after *Herself Surprised*. It is in many ways the most complex of the three novels. As the oldest of the three protagonists, Thomas Wilcher's is the longest of the three lives and the most explicitly and consciously, even self-consciously, ruminative of Cary's speaking voices. At his most dogmatic moments in the novel, Cary is intrusive, compelling Wilcher into situations and actions that bear out Cary's thesis that the conservative man, "who loves his old home, his old fields, and the old ways," is doomed to suffer the loss of all of those things he most cherishes, because of the "continuous revolution in which . . . we are compelled" to live. But when Wilcher is allowed to be himself and not the banner for a thesis, he emerges as a fascinating character, perverse, multifaceted, and intensely alive.

Cary's critics and reviewers have been less inclined to consider the problems presented by *To Be A Pilgrim* than they have those of the other two books, perhaps because Sara lends herself so well to comparison with other great female characters in the literature of the past. *The Horse's Mouth,* on the other hand, has such a richness of Blake quotation that one can rummage around in it happily for a long time without exhausting the material. There are no such convenient handles or evasions available for Thomas Wilcher's tale. The novel is also intensely compacted and inward pointing. In addition, there is the possibility that Wilcher may be mad, a situation that leads Bloom to write that "there is almost no end to the ambiguity that Cary has lodged in this second volume of his trilogy."[11]

But the story has great power and, as an example of the novelist's art, may be the best of the three novels. Gulley and Sara are such flagrant characters that their individuality and style do much to carry the stories in which they appear, but Wilcher lacks their charismatic charm. In fact, an important aspect of his personality is its surface dullness, a fact of which he is fully aware. Throughout the novel Wilcher contrasts himself, usually unfavorably, with the other characters who flood its pages, emphasizing their characters and through them coming to understand his own. The result of these continual interchanges, reflections, backtracks, and musings is a density of context that creates a solid, three-dimensional world within the novel.

The physical center of the novel is Tolbrook, Wilcher's family estate, which has been in the family for generations and comes to his brother, Edward, and then, on Edward's death, to Wilcher. Tolbrook embodies everything that has given meaning to Wilcher's life, and as he prepares for death, he hopes to draw it around him like a familiar comforter, but that hope is dashed by the swift changes that are visited on his beloved house.

Wilcher's major emotional relationships are with his sister, Lucy, and his brothers, Edward and William and their wives, mistresses, and lovers. Outside of the family, Wilcher becomes involved with Julie and Sara, but Julie is gone by the time the story opens and Sara comes late into Wilcher's life. Although he insists that he loves Sara and values her, Wilcher allows her to be taken from him and arrested and finally sent to prison. While she is in prison, he writes letters to her that he never mails. Dying, he really has no time for anything but getting his own life into some sort of perspective and attempting, at last, to be what he has all his life wished to be, a pilgrim.

The title of the story is drawn from a verse in a Blake hymn, "who would true valor see, / Let him come hither. / All here will constant be / come wind, come weather. / There's no discouragement / shall make him once repent / His first avowed intent, / To be a Pilgrim." Wilcher is a double pilgrim. He is a seeker into the past for the meanings of his own life and a Christian pilgrim attempting to make his soul. He is a kind of exemplar of Christ's warning that only by losing one's life shall it be saved. Foster sees a similarity between Thomas Wilcher and Prufrock, who share many anxieties and timidities. He also sees another connection with Eliot in the line from *The Waste Land*: "These fragments I have shored against my ruin." Throughout his life Wilcher attempts to pull around him "fragments" of the created world in order to preserve them from "ruin" and himself among them. Perhaps this lifelong effort is a third pilgrimage, a failed one, and one which he finally abandons.

Giles Mitchell finds a connection between *To Be A Pilgrim* and Chaucer's "Man of Law's Tale." Like the Man of Law, who is redeemed by the story he tells, Wilcher is also redeemed through art, through his tale.[12] The story makes many other literary references, among them to *Beowulf, Piers Plowman,* Chaucer, Bunyan, Austen, Wagner, Priestly, Whistler, Ibsen, and Trollope.[13] Mitchell finds a major theme in the novel in *The Pilgrim's Progress,* when Pilgrim says to Apollyon, "Rejoice not against me, O Mine Enemy! When I fall I shall rise." And as if the proliferation of literary reference has no end in the novel, there is a further connection between Wilcher and Shakespeare's Prospero, who, explaining art, speaks of "the

baseless fabric of this vision," and, "an unsubstantial pageant." Wilcher
refers to Tolbrook as "Platonic forms" and says later, that "civilization is a
fabric hanging in the air" (*P,* 237, 295).[14]

Wilcher adds to the welter of literary reference by constantly quoting
his brother Edward's poetry, seventy-seven lines in all.[15] Edward's poetry
is written in couplets, reminiscent of Pope, and expresses a satirical view of
existence and men's morals and motives that Wilcher cannot accept, can
scarcely understand, because he cannot enter into his brother's way of
regarding life, which is that of a gentleman who places his own pleasure
first in life. Edward is tolerant of Wilcher and amused by his sister, Lucy,
but he throws away a brilliant career by choosing to take a holiday on the
Continent at just the wrong moment. At least, he does not regret that
action.

It is a fair question to ask how Cary manages under the burden of such
diverse references to make Wilcher a coherent character. The answer may
lie in Cary's manipulation of Tolbrook in the novel, which Mitchell calls
"one of the most remarkable symbols in modern fiction." Another critic
has called it England, although it is certainly not England in the sense that
Howards End is England in E. M. Forster's novel of that name; whereas
Howards End is menaced by an encroaching London sprawl, Tolbrook
Manor is being destroyed by Heraclitean change, working through the
agency of time. The major importance of Tolbrook to the novel is made
clear at the beginning of the story. It is to be the vehicle of Wilcher's
self-exploration: "I was excited by the thought of exploring the old house,
after so many years. I opened all doors to these memories, from which, in
my late mental anxiety, I had fled, and at once my whole body like
Tolbrook itself was full of strange quick sensations. My veins seemed to
rustle with mice, and my brain, like Tolbrook's roof, let in daylight at a
thousand crevices" (*P,* 6).

The occasion of this awakening is Wilcher's forced return to Tolbrook
under the care of his young niece, Ann, daughter of his dead brother,
Edward. She is a doctor and has taken over his care as an alternative to his
being confined in an asylum. The return to Tolbrook occurs a month after
Sara is sent to prison. Wilcher says that he "was very ill on account of this
disaster." In fact, under stress, he reverted to an old tendency that had
been brought under control by his relationship with Sara, exposing
himself in parks and on the street to young women. The police become
involved and the family is obliged to act on his behalf.

Wilcher is taken back to Tolbrook to die. Calmed by Ann's care and the
rejuvenating influences of Tolbrook, Wilcher enters into a new and vital

relationship with his past, through which he makes a second pilgrimage in search of grace. The novel thus takes its shape from Wilcher's reflections. And while it is possible to trace several story lines through the pages of the book, the center of interest, from first to last, is the encounter between Wilcher's remembering mind and the memories that present themselves to him.

Lucy.   Wilcher continually refers to Lucy as the person who has presented him with one of the most vital relationships in his life. Like Sara, Lucy Wilcher is a woman who possesses a natural faith that Wilcher envies and desires to possess (*P,* 48). But Lucy's resemblance to Sara stops with the common ground of natural piety, for Lucy is a rebel through and through. She has not the slightest trace of nest-builder in her, and she lives by defiance.

Cary succeeds admirably, particularly in the early descriptions of Lucy, in creating a character set apart by her courage, intelligence, and intensity. When she is twelve, she challenges her father's authority in such a way that neither can escape the challenge. As Wilcher says in describing the confrontation, "she challenged him, with all the cunning of her malice, her devil, to a final battle of wills, counting as she always did, in all her battles, upon the very virtues of the enemy to help her destroy him and triumph over him. She said in effect, 'You can kill me, if you dare; or own that you don't dare, and submit to me'" (*P,* 34).

Lucy is Cary's prototypical bitch-goddess. In saying that he feels her "woman's malice" neither Wilcher nor Cary (at least explicitly) pause to define the nature of that malice. But the evidence has been accumulating through a dozen novels that for Cary the malice is clearly the woman's drive to power, in particular the ignorant woman's unreflective drive, which emerges out of her female temperament and is expressed through her will. Elizabeth in *The African Witch* is such a woman. So is Ruth, the older sister in *The Moonlight.* It is an extensive sisterhood in the novels, and the trails of these bitch-goddesses are strewn with dead and dying men. Lucy's conflict with their father comes as a result of her quarrel with a new governess, a gentle young woman whom Wilcher describes as "a fair, pretty mild creature . . . musical and clever and, I think, rather High Church." Lucy despises her and in a characteristic act of scorn tosses one of the governess's holy pictures into the chamber pot. Mr. Wilcher learns of this double iniquity, which combines "blasphemy with indecency" and determines to thrash Lucy with a cane, the standard family punishment for serious breaches of decorum in the nursery.

Lucy takes this beating, not in good grace but with her usual refusal to repent. She screams and fights and behaves as rebelliously as possible. That evening Lucy refuses to attend family prayers. When sent for, she announces that she will never again attend prayers or attend church, her reason being that "she hated God, who was nothing but an old Jew" (*P*, 35). Her father then orders her to appear, which she refuses to do, saying that she "did not care for anybody or for anything they said to her." Wilcher sees at once that Lucy is defying the father and counting on the fact that he has already beaten her once during the day and will not care to do it again. He also sees Lucy is "counting precisely on that point to defeat him." The confrontation is between Lucy and patriarchal authority, root and branch, God and father.

Mr. Wilcher determines to act consistently. That is to say, he has a very high code for women and "coarseness and brutality in a woman was to him a sin against Nature, as well as his code. He thought of women as the guardians of a special virtue given them by God. . . . Lucy's crime was unnatural in a woman, and he beat her severely" (*P*, 35). A few moments after the beating ends, Wilcher, terrified by Lucy's defiance, sees his sister come flying down the stairs, "her eyes wide open and staring front of her like a lunatic," her face, "white as a candle." As she runs, she tears at her clothes. Once out of the house, she heads at full speed for a small pond near the house. Rending her clothes into rags as she rushes forward, she plunges into the pond and vanishes beneath the surface. She cannot swim and neither can Wilcher.

Wilcher begins to scream, attracting the attention of a gardener, who rushes into the water and fishes Lucy out. Once out of the muddy water, she begins to throw up and shout, "He can't hurt me—never—never," referring directly to her father and, perhaps, more generally to God. Set on her feet, Lucy bolts again into the pond, only to be dragged out again by the astonished gardener, while she screams, "I will—I will."

The episode is very important to the story, and to the entire canon of Cary's fiction. Lucy's wild defiance is later treated as a family joke: "Remember the day Lucy was beaten twice?" But there is nothing at all laughable about the episode. Lucy deliberately precipitates the fight with her father for the express purpose of smashing his authority. When she fails to carry out her intention, she breaks out in an even more lunatic rage and attempts to drown herself. Only with difficulty is she prevented from doing so.

Her defiance of her father, of male authority, and her malice, mentioned by her brother earlier, are central to her character. It is her aggression that, thwarted in one endeavor, only breaks out in another. Remembering her, Wilcher says, "the very idea of Lucy goes to my head. 'There aren't any such people nowadays,' I think. 'And what if she had a devil? She did

God's work. Out of devilry. She made something good and noble of her life' " (*P,* 40). But does she? It makes more sense to say that she simply goes from an act of destruction to one of self-destruction; and it says a great deal for Cary's view of things that he manages to be so consistent in presenting her life during the remainder of the novel.

Wilcher thinks that his sister has had a satisfying life. She does not marry within her class but runs off with an evangelist named Brown, who is the head of a grubby sect calling themselves Benjamites. Brown marries her but reduces her to a drudge, abuses her, humiliates her, takes other women into her bed, and makes her serve them. She loses her looks and her health, but she persists in her degradation with all the determination that she brought to her efforts to drown herself. Her acts, her brother says, were set off by "a devil's whim, but it flew straight forward, it broke a way through walls. And now I think, 'How did Lucy know at twenty-one, even in her whims, what I don't know till now from all of my books, that the way to a satisfying life, a good life, is through an act of faith and courage' " (*P,* 47–48).

In the end, Lucy comes home to Tolbrook to die. She is not yet sixty when she dies of a kidney disease that is curable but which she will not treat or allow to be treated. Wilcher says that when she died a "virtue had gone from me and the house." He and his sister fought hard and loved one another intensely all of their lives. But to the end of her life, the only men she ever respects are her father, who beats her, and Brown, who also beats her and humiliates her. And it is Brown, whom she calls "the master," who "threw a glory on the whole world" for her.

Edward.   Edward is Thomas Wilcher's older brother. Through him a dark thread is woven into the novel, not only with the near-tragic events of Edward's life but also with the tortuous relationship between Wilcher and his brilliant older brother. By the workings of English law, Edward inherits Tolbrook and the family wealth. Wilcher, who had dreamed as a young man of becoming a missionary, is compelled to take to the law to support himself. Edward, meanwhile, begins to have a career in politics and to live the life of a country gentleman.

As a character Edward bears a close resemblance to the father in Cary's earlier *A House of Children.* Edward is an eighteenth-century man, embodying those values which Cary associated with that period. Edward pleases himself, has a highly developed love of the arts, enjoys intelligent women, and regards "living well" as the first duty of his life, perhaps the only duty. He is quite content to allow his brother Thomas to look after the business of running Tolbrook while he concentrates on spending his inheritance on travel, clothes, wine, his club, and women.

The war comes and Wilcher is sent to France as a stretcher-bearer. Edward becomes an officer and remains in the army for some time after the end of the war, seemingly unable to find his way back into civilian life. Tolbrook is now mortgaged and remortgaged and when he does come out of the army, Edward is obliged to live quietly. His wife, disgusted with his failure, leaves him. Wilcher uses every opportunity to drive Edward into a full realization of the extent of his extravagances and to insert himself more and more absolutely into the life of Tolbrook. In the end Edward catches an influenza and dies cheerfully of the ensuing pneumonia, leaving behind him a daughter, Ann, the niece who will become Wilcher's keeper.

Wilcher never understands his brother, but does come to acknowledge that in many things, such as the war's approach, for example, Edward was right and he wrong. But he is never able to grasp the vision of life that Edward possesses, although he glimpses it from time to time throughout the novel by means of Edward's bitter and often humorous couplets, which Wilcher quotes. He probably misses entirely the irony in Edward's last remark to him, "You knew what you wanted, Tommy, and you made for it, from the beginning. It's the only way. The new age can only use specialists" (*P,* 280). Edward's sense of humor is a part of that vision that Wilcher cannot grasp.

William. Wilcher's second brother belongs to a category of human beings that used to be called the hewers of wood and drawers of water. Bill, as he is called in the novel, is something of a family joke. Early in life he enters the army and follows his career to India and the East, returning home to find a wife and gratefully accepting the one the family provides. Wilcher says of Bill's marriage to Amy that both are "simple-minded persons" and therefore expect to love one another and to be happy. In fact, they do love each other and they are happy (*P,* 98). It becomes a Wilcher ritual to laugh at Amy and Bill, who are prone to get into trouble and yet emerge from it relatively unscathed.

As the novel slowly works through the periods of Wilcher's life, actually moving from the present backward through time and then forward to the present again, Cary tells the story of each of the principal characters, establishing their relationships to Wilcher and showing how their lives impinge on Wilcher's own. By the time the story has reached the present, only Wilcher, his niece Ann, and Amy remain of those closest to him. He is cut off from Sara, and with Lucy's death, Amy fades from the scene, her never very clearly defined task in the novel completed.

Tolbrook.   No consideration of the influences working on Wilcher would be complete without an acknowledgment of the lifelong obsession that Wilcher has for Tolbrook, the house that is at once his home, his ideal of life, and his earthly paradise. Wilcher's hope through much of the novel is to preserve Tolbrook exactly as he has always known it. For many years he manages to keep the estate functioning, despite the gradually increasing neglect that Edward's extravagances force upon it.

By the time Wilcher comes back to Tolbrook, however, in the keeping of his niece, Ann, the house and its lands are deteriorating. Robert returns to Tolbrook at this time too. The son of Lucy and Brown, he has been in South America for several years, and on his return he begins the task of restoring Tolbrook to prosperity by means of scientific farming. He also establishes a relationship with Ann that leads to an unsatisfactory marriage.

Wilcher is at first pleased with Robert's eagerness to take over the place and make it into an economic success. He sees in his mind's eye the old Tolbrook restored. But no such thing occurs. The old Tolbrook, a place of winding lanes, small fields bounded by dense hedges, where every foot of ground and every tree and lane is redolent with memories for Wilcher, is to be swept away. Hedges are to be grubbed, lanes obliterated, and the trees cast down in order that the fields can be put together and worked with machines. This change strikes Wilcher with the force of a devastation and nearly kills him.

The finishing piece of destruction that does, indeed, bring to an end Wilcher's dependence on Tolbrook is Robert's decision to use the Adams drawing room for a threshing room. It is a huge and beautiful room, built in accordance with the Adams's design, with cupids on the ceiling, fireplaces, and intricate scroll work. Into this architectural triumph Robert moves a huge threshing machine, which crushes the frames of the French doors as it is forced into the room. Then he starts the motor and the whole house shakes with the power of its vast engine. The threshing begins, safe from the consequences of the falling barometer that has threatened the harvest. Wilcher sits down to watch the threshing and says, "I have surrendered because I cannot fight and now it seems to me that not change but life has lifted me and carried me forward on the stream. It is but a new life that flows through the old house; and like all

life, part of that sustaining power which is the oldest thing in the world"
(*P,* 328).

In his book Wilcher often remarks that as he is approaching death he
must make his soul, meaning that he must discover in what relationship
he stands to his God. Is he successful? The answer, probably, is yes. Early
in the story, Wilcher is reading the family prayers to Ann, her new baby,
and the nurse, when the words he is speaking suddenly seize him. "Now
though I had begun to read in a spirit of formal duty, to improve the
occasion, the words took hold of me and carried me into grace. They
opened for me, if I may speak so, a window upon the landscape of
eternity wherein I saw the form of things, love and birth and death,
change and fall, in their eternal kinds" (*P,* 121). He continues his
reading with difficulty and finally is so moved by his feelings that he
weeps and cannot finish the prayers.

This episode brings us as close as Cary is prepared to come to the
process by which Thomas Wilcher seeks his salvation. But the sudden
vision, in a slightly altered form, comes upon Wilcher again at the close
of the novel as he lies in bed recuperating from another failing of his
heart:

As I lie with nothing to do but feel the world agitating round my bed, not only
the fields of this house are present to my mind's eye but the moor, the
Longwater, Queensport, and beyond them all the villages and towns of this
country. . . . I walk upon the fields of the whole island as upon my own carpet,
and I feel the same exasperation against them for being a perpetual burden on my
regard. . . . For I know very well they are not being properly looked after. I love
this Island as I loved Tolbrook; and I tremble for it; and perhaps I shall be happy
to get some peace from both of them. They have broken my heart between them.
(*P,* 341)

Wilcher determines to die leaving no will so that Tolbrook will be
divided equally among his survivors, and his final request is to be buried
without a coffin in Tolbrook churchyard, in order that his body may
mingle more swiftly with his beloved English earth. Wilcher manages to
break through the limitations of character which Cary had originally
established for him. He is more than the timid, humorless conservative
man. His love for Tolbrook becomes a more general love for his people
and his land. He most certainly makes his soul and in so doing emerges as
one of Cary's most complex and attractive characters.

The Horse's Mouth

The Horse's Mouth is certainly the best known of Cary's novels. It is also
the one that has received the most critical attention and praise, being
generally regarded as Cary's masterpiece and a major work of twentieth-
century fiction. Interest in the book stems, no doubt, from the remarkable portrait of Gulley Jimson, who is the book's protagonist, and the
astonishingly high level of energy that gives the reader the impression of
being flung forward by the narrative at a breakneck pace. The book's
popularity has also been enhanced by the excellent film which was made
of the novel, starring Alec Guiness in the role of Gulley Jimson.

Cary began writing *The Horse's Mouth* in November 1942, the year
after the publication of *Herself Surprised* and the same year as the publication of *To Be A Pilgrim*. Cary had gone to Edinburgh in November 1942
at the invitation of John Dover Wilson of Edinburgh University to give a
lecture entitled "Tolstoi on Art and Morals." Riding home on the train
from that visit he "had some ideas about a new book." The book was *The
Horse's Mouth*. Foster writes that the fact that Cary had begun the story
"on the train back from Edinburgh, tired, cold and wedged into a
compartment full of soldiers, shows how deeply he had been affected by
the memories of his own painting days in that city."[16]

Soon after his return to Oxford, Cary set off again, this time for Africa,
to make a film that would be used as a morale booster for the public and,
perhaps, those in the various services. He was fortunate during the voyage
out in having for his cabin mate the cameraman, Desmond Dickinson, a
cockney who provided Cary with a rich fund of slang and idiom and local
knowledge about London that Cary passed along to Gulley. The manuscript came off the ship with Cary, and when Cary's party were stranded
in Freetown, Sierra Leone, waiting for a flight to Tanganyika, Cary
worked steadily on it. It took him two years to complete the novel and
see it through to publication.[17]

His own attitude toward the book, at least in its initial stages, was
mixed. Writing to his wife, he told her that he thought it would "be a
damned queer book. . . ." He shared the fear with his publisher, who
encouraged him to write what he liked. So he wrote the novel, drawing
heavily on his youthful experiences as an art student as well as on the
knowledge of those artist friends in and near Oxford who were willing to
give him advice on questions of technique and so on.

Without actually saying that Sir Stanley Spencer, an artist famous for
his immense canvasses of resurrection scenes, was the model for Gulley

Jimson, Foster does point out that like Gulley, Spencer distorted the human form for his own purposes and laced his conversation with a flow of quotations from the Bible and William Blake.[18] Other artists contributed to Gulley as a character as well. Augustus John, Henry Moore, and Gilbert Spencer all contributed. Some of the poorer artists Cary invited into his home actually stole ivory carvings off his mantlepiece, thus providing him with material for one episode in the novel. Cary was tolerant of these thefts, saying that they were a result of the artists' pride which prevented them from asking for money. Whatever their motives in lifting the carvings, their acts have gained a kind of notorious permanence in the pages of Cary's novel.

Writing of *The Horse's Mouth* and more particularly of Gulley, Cary has described Jimson as "the original genius," whose tragedy is that "the conservatives fight him and destroy him." Cary here oversimplifies the events in the novel, as he does the action of *To Be A Pilgrim* and perhaps also *Herself Surprised*. Pointing out that Gulley is destroyed because his opponents resist his new ideas, knowing how dangerous they are to their "achieved worlds," Cary reduces the struggle in *The Horse's Mouth* to a contest between two factions who know what they are doing. Had this been all there is to the novel, it would never have enjoyed the success it has had from its first appearance. Looking back at his novel, Cary is less generous to its achievement than he ought to have been.

Cary's faint praise of the book may be due less to modesty than to a sense that his first trilogy, brought to a close with *The Horse's Mouth*, was a failure. Cary was not unhappy with the individual volumes of the trilogy but, rather, with the three as a whole. In the prefatory note to the *First Trilogy*, he writes that he failed to bring the three worlds of the novels into conjunction. "They were not," he wrote, "sufficiently interlocked to give the richness and depth of actuality that I had hoped for."[19] In the second trilogy he attempted to overcome this limitation by confining himself to a single subject, politics.

In one important sense, Cary's estimate of what had occurred in the first trilogy is valid. *The Horse's Mouth* is a novel that stands alone. It is not dependent at all on *To Be A Pilgrim* and scarcely more on *Herself Surprised*. Having read the two earlier novels the reader does bring to *The Horse's Mouth* a developed understanding of Sara and Gulley, but it is at least arguable that the Sara and Gulley of *Herself Surprised* and *To Be A Pilgrim* are different characters from those with the same names in the two earlier novels. This does not mean that their personalities are different. It means that they are removed by time and circumstances from what they were in their earlier incarnations. It is also important to note that there is no development in the two characters in the sense that the reader finds Gulley and Sara in *The Horse's Mouth* living lives that are the consequences of their personalities, seen developing over the span of two previous novels.

Cary would, perhaps, argue that character in the novels is, indeed, the dominant force at work. He would rightly point out, as he insists in the prefatory note to *Herself Surprised,* that when faced with a choice he always placed character first. But, to emphasize a point made earlier, Cary uses the word "character" in a special way. In the case of Sara and Gulley and Thomas Wilcher, too, for that matter, he means by "character" a fixed state of being, an unvarying mode of existence. Sara is the nest-builder, Gulley is the creative artist who destroys in order to create, and Wilcher is the conservative man, struggling to hold together a house being shaken to pieces by the earthquake of change.

As the word has been more frequently used from the time of Samuel Richardson in the eighteenth century, character in a work of fiction is something emergent, almost a process, that is, subject to modification under the pressure of events. There are two great roads by which characters have traveled in English fiction, self-expression and compromise. Jude Fawley in Thomas Hardy's *Jude the Obscure* is an example of a character seeking to fulfill himself and, in his case, failing; Elizabeth Bennett in Jane Austen's *Pride and Prejudice* is an example of a character learning to compromise her drive to self-assertion. Cary's characters, however, follow neither of these two roads. They simply do not change. They are immune to growth, know nothing of the mastery of motivation, and remain frozen in their fixed design. It is in this sense that Sara and Gulley are not conventional characters and do not in *The Horse's Mouth* bring to fulfillment a process of growth begun in the first volume of the trilogy.

The Story.   *The Horse's Mouth,* though rich in event, is not a novel of action. The plot is not particularly gripping. Gulley is the center of the reader's interest throughout the story. The action opens with Gulley's returning to his boat-house studio after having been released from jail and attempting to pick up the pieces of his life. Old and poor, he must connive to find the materials to go on painting. Following some adventures that land him in prison again, he makes his way into the home of the wealthy Beeders, who endure his drunken presence through dinner and then go away on a holiday, forgetting all about him.

But Gulley reenters their flat and sets about painting his Lazarus painting on one of their walls, supporting himself and a sculptor, who also moves in, by pawning the Beeders' belongings. The painting is never finished, and Gulley flees London to escape arrest. He eventually makes his way back to London and, finding a deserted chapel, begins painting yet another picture. Told to leave the building by the local authorities, he refuses. A bulldozer knocks down the wall on which he is working and he suffers a stroke. The reader discovers that Gulley has been telling his story to one of the sisters in a hospital and is talking only because he can no longer paint.

Although there are a host of minor incidents built into the tale, incidents which bring in Sara, grown old and terribly fat, Hickson, Gulley's one-time patron, Old Plant, an old friend, and Nosy, a young admirer whom Gulley tries in vain to dissuade from becoming an artist, the organizing principle of the novel is the four visions which come to Jimson in the course of the novel.[20] The first two visions occur while Gulley is still working on, or at least thinking about, his painting, *The Fall,* and lead him to consider doing another painting, *The Creation.*

His third vision involves "Old Diamond Death" Spinoza, who throughout this novel serves as a foil to the image of the creative artist. Mitchell makes a good case for seeing Spinoza as a representative of the rational, ordered vision of life contrasted with "the divine fecundity of the artist."[21] It is also possible that Spinoza serves to contrast with Blake, whose poem "The Mental Traveller" exerts a profound hold on Gulley's imagination.

Gulley's fourth vision gives rise to his uncompleted painting, *The Raising of Lazarus,* begun and left uncompleted in Beeder's apartment. The last painting on which Gulley works in the novel is *The Creation.* It is the greatest and most ambitious of the three paintings undertaken and results from his second vision, in which he sees the Fall in terms of generation rather than destruction.[22] The four visions move Gulley steadily forward toward a more and more positive identification with the generative forces of life. His *Creation* painting is to be a final great affirmation of this theme of generation, but, as is the case with all of his paintings in the novel, he fails to complete it.

Mitchell insists that the reader is "never to forget that Jimson's constant search for new forms is simultaneously a search for meaning . . . all of which derive from his basically spiritual view of art and reality."[23] These "meanings," however, elude Jimson and hence also the reader. We are left with feet and a whale's eye and burning towers amid a jumble of other images mentioned by Gulley as he muses over the wreck of his paintings. In a general sense, however, we do not need these paintings in a finished form to understand that their cumulative meanings are essentially the meaning of the novel itself, which is that the creative force of life, expressed through Gulley Jimson, is both destructive and creative, the creation emerging out of the destruction, the way, as Mitchell points out, the *Creation* painting emerges out of Gulley's murder of Sara. The reason, or at least a reason, why none of Gulley's paintings is ever finished is that creation itself, which they come to stand for, is not finished, may never be finished.

Limitations of space prevent a detailed analysis here of the uses to which art is put in the novel. In *The Art Theme in Joyce Cary's First Trilogy*, Giles Mitchell's discussion of the function of art in the novels is exhaustive and persuasive without pretending to be the final statement on the matter. For a key to the Blake materials in *The Horse's Mouth*, Andrew Wright's *Joyce Cary: A Preface to His Novels* is particularly useful, providing identification of all of the Blake passages and a complete text of "The Mental Traveller," a Blake poem on which Cary relies heavily in the novel. Although the Blake quotations play a conspicuous role in the novel, they do not constitute a particularly difficult element in the writing.

The Blake with whom Cary is concerned is the visionary, whose version of the original fall from grace is not that of man's falling away from God through an abridgment of God's law but the fall of primal man, who is himself God, who embodies the universe. Primal or Universal Man, as Blake calls him, "fell" through division, making the Creation the real fall and not Adam and Eve's eating the apple. When nature was created out of chaos, primal man found himself sharing in the division that is the present fallen state of the cosmos.

Blake's interpretation of the redemption is equally personal. The redeemer is not Christ in Blake's mythology but the human imagination as it is embodied most particularly in the poet, the artist. What has to be redeemed is the condition of opposites, which came naturally into being when man fell from unity to differentiation. It is in this sense that dual existence of the tiger and the lamb is to be understood and the apparent contradiction that the artist, in order to create, must destroy as he moves progressively toward the unification of his vision, sweeping away those hindrances to his reunifying drive as he goes. Gulley's visions become increasingly inclusive as the novel progresses, and he defends the murder of Sara on the grounds that she is trying to put him in her "placket pocket," that is, to hold him in division.

Essentially, Cary's use of Blake is summarized in the novel's title, *The Horse's Mouth*. Presumably, if the horse tells you how to place your bet, you are getting the best advice there is. Blake's artist has access to his imagination, which is the horse's mouth, the medium through which Unity expresses its eternal essense. Gulley certainly accepts the Blakean proposition that the artist stands at the living center of creation, spinning its unending forms. His story exists because he can no longer paint and is but one more expression of the creativity of the divine spirit in the artist.

The nearly fifty Blake quotations in the novel provide Gulley with his inspiration and insight into the meaning of life, as well as supplying justification for his actions. In a wider sense, Gulley is accounted for by the Blakean vision which Cary bends to his purposes in the novel. In particular, "The Mental Traveller," combined with Gulley's rather self-serving reading of the poem, reveal to him the pattern of life and his relationship to it. In the reading Sara becomes "the woman old," or necessity, who seeks to nail down the artist and imprison him. Whether or not the reader is prepared to accept Gulley's reading of the poem, Wright is convincing in finding the poem central to an understanding of the novel.

Meaning in the novel is not confined to that which emerges from the art theme in the novel. Easily overlooked in the novel are two subplots which carry much of the story's meaning. The first is Jenny's story. Jenny is Gulley's sister, and he refers to her unhappy life at various times in the course of the novel. Jenny runs away with a thirty-five-year-old man who mistreats her until she loses her beauty and who then abandons her. Soon afterwards, she commits suicide, a victim of the world's injustice. Plant's is the second story; he too is a victim of injustice. By losing his thumb, he loses his trade and his ability to support himself, and is thrown back on charity and the doss house.

That injustice is a concomitant of existence is one of the meanings of the novel and one which Gulley articulates from time to time in the course of telling his tale. Gulley's own burning sense of this injustice constantly threatens to break out in rage, rage which he rightly resists, aware that to surrender to it might well kill him. It does land him in jail when, for instance, succumbing to his anger over Hickson's jobbing him, he steals the snuff boxes and netsukes and pitches them through

Hickson's drawing room windows (*HM,* 100). It nearly brings on a stroke when he is with Nosy at the bus stop and getting into a ferment over the government and its follies: "But I saw the danger in time. And I said, 'Hold me up, Nosy, and keep cool. No malice intended. Revenge has a green face, he feeds on corpses'" (*HM,* 211). And, of course, he drives off his anger at having his *Creation* destroyed and his body fail him by saying, at the conclusion of his story, "I should laugh all round my neck at this minute if my shirt wasn't a bit on the tight side." The nun beside him tells him he would do better to pray, to which he replies, "'Same thing, mother.'"

Chapter Seven
The Political Trilogy

It is inevitable that readers coming to the second trilogy from the first will make comparisons between Sara Monday and Nina Woodville as the vital centers of their fictional worlds. At first glance, the possibility of making useful comparisons between these very different characters appears slim. Nina is a member of the upper middle class, monied, intelligent, and well educated. Sara, by contrast, belongs to the working class. She is poor and comes equipped with a kind of native shrewdness that substitutes for intelligence.

So much for the difference. Careful reading will reveal, however, important similarities between Nina and Sara; and an understanding of these similarities will help to make clear what Cary is doing in both trilogies. The differences between the two characters, which appear to separate them by so wide a gulf, are, in actuality, merely superficial. In fact, Nina and Sara are truly sisters under the skin.

Their roles are very much alike. They are, first, interesting characters in themselves with interesting stories to tell about themselves. More importantly, they are unifying forces in both trilogies. In this respect, Nina is of more importance than Sara, who plays a marginal role in *To Be A Pilgrim* and *The Horse's Mouth,* although she is inspiration and catalyst in both novels. Nina is dealt with peripherally in her trilogy only in *Except The Lord,* and even here she is present in the reader's mind because he knows that it is to Nina that Chester may be dictating this memoir. In *Prisoner of Grace* and *Not Honour More* she is absolutely essential to the stories, because the first is an account of her life while the second receives direction largely because of her.

A second important aspect of the similarity between Nina and Sara is their common fatality, the certainty of their martyrdom. Both die violent deaths, murdered by the men they love. Whatever shift in focus Cary seeks in the second trilogy, he remains consistent with the earlier trilogy in this respect. Both women are blood sacrifices to the obsessions of the men to whom they have given their hearts. Sara dies because Gulley needs money with which to continue painting, and Nina dies because the crazed Jim Latter believes that by killing her he will halt the advance of corruption in public life. Nina and Sara are killed in the name of abstractions in which neither believes. Ostensibly, Nina is sacrificed to Honor and Sara to Art; but, in truth, they are sacrificed to the inflamed egos of the men who murder them.

Throughout their lives, their needs and expectations are considered only after the needs of their men are filled. Sara is never allowed to establish the home she longs for. Nina never escapes the prisons in which Chester and Jim place her, and twice in the trilogy she attempts suicide as a desperate remedy to her humiliating situation. Although the action of the trilogies bears out the awful fatality in which Nina and Sara are trapped, Cary never acknowledges its existence, not in exposition, in the words of other characters, or in the consciousness of the female characters themselves. It is as though he was not aware of what he has done to them or knew and thought it unworthy of mention. As a consequence, it is impossible to say with any certainty whether Cary thought of Nina and Sara as representing women in general or only as aspects of the fictional worlds in which he placed them. But because what happens to them is so much a part of what happens to all of Cary's female characters, it is difficult not to conclude that he saw women like Sara and Nina as handmaidens, nest-builders, and victims.

The second trilogy is generally characterized as Cary's political trilogy. Cary consciously developed the political aspect of the novels. He was quite clear about what he wished to do. He had given a sketch of what he intended in one of Edward's speeches in *To Be A Pilgrim* which complains that political novels do not give a sense of "real politics," "of moles digging frantically about to dodge some unknown noise overhead. . . . You don't get the sense of limitation and confusion. . . . I should like to do for politics what Tolstoi did for war—show what a muddle and confusion it is, and that it must always be a muddle and confusion where good men are wasted and destroyed simply by luck as by a chance bullet" (*P,* 266–67). After completing the trilogy one wonders if it is not a good woman rather than a good man who is destroyed. Certainly, one will wonder whether Cary meant Jim or Chester to be the good man of Edward's speech.

Actually, the second trilogy was not Cary's first effort to treat politics in his fiction. In a very real sense, he dealt with it in all of his African novels and in none more than in the incompleted Cock Jarvis story. Jim

Latter has many of Jarvis's characteristics and shares many of his experiences. Cary had dealt with political matters in his nonfiction beginning with *Power In Men* (1939) and later in *The Case for African Freedom* (1941) and *British West Africa* (1946). In a broad sense he also deals with political matters in *Castle Corner* and *Charley is My Darling*.

More specifically, the political trilogy deals with the public career of Chester Nimmo from his childhood through the period of the General Strike in the spring of 1926 and the death of Chester and Nina. The three novels attempt to represent the shape of politics in the modern democracies in both their public and private dimensions. The public aspect of the condition is shown through the careers of Chester and Jim, while the private dimension is presented through the marriages between Nina and Chester and Nina and Jim. Cary also touches on such issues as the growth of unions as political power centers, the relationship of the law to social justice, and the conflict between private perceptions of truth and honor, and the pressure of public necessity to compromise those values in the interest of preserving peace.

Prisoner of Grace

Cary began *Prisoner of Grace* in April 1949, one of many works in progress in the year of his wife's death. Cary had written to a friend some months before beginning *Prisoner of Grace* that he had seventeen novels in progress.[1] It took him two years to write the novel, and he did not deliver the completed manuscript to the publishers until the spring of 1952 after delays resulting from the loss of a page and the misnumbering of chapters. He seemed to be unable to deal with such details in the absence of his wife and may, indeed, have been reacting against her loss by refusing to cope efficiently.

According to Nina, this first volume in the trilogy is written because certain "revelations" are to be published, in which her life and that of Chester Nimmo are to come under hostile scrutiny by writers bent on discrediting Nimmo and herself. Nina's opening statement in the novel provides a point of view that is sustained throughout the story. But her defense of Nimmo is also an indictment of him and a revelation of her own character. The first person device serves admirably to give immediacy and urgency to Nina's recital and through the use of parentheses becomes a flexible vehicle of Nina's personality and its tragic contradictions. Cary's use of these brackets, as he called them in the English fashion, came in for harsh criticism; but, considering the success of the strategy, their use has to be seen as a technical triumph.

Surprisingly, the novel begins in the classic fashion of a romance. The reader is introduced to Nina Woodville, an orphan, living with her Aunt Latter in a kind of elegant bondage, with no idea of who she is or what she ought to do with her life. The decision is effectively taken out of her hands when, at the age of seventeen, she becomes pregnant by Aunt Latter's nephew, James Latter; because he cannot marry her without losing his position in his regiment, she is forced by her aunt into a marriage of convenience with the rising young politician, Chester Nimmo. So, although the novel opens as a romance, the form is subverted. Nina is trapped and the story unfolds as a record of her efforts to free herself from her unwanted marriage and to make a life with Jim, the man we are told she has always loved. The romance is further subverted when Nina does finally escape from Nimmo and marries Jim but is unable to separate herself completely from Chester. In the end her vacillation leads to her death. Jim murders her.

In the prefatory essay written for the novel, Cary says that the story is called *Prisoner of Grace* because "Nina was held to her husband by her sense that he was on the whole a good man" and that she did not wish to destroy his career by exposing him to the scandal of a divorce. Cary's explanation is not altogether satisfying. Nina repeatedly says that she regards Chester as a great man who was doing important, even vital, work for the country. And when she has finally divorced him and married Jim, she defends her decision to allow Chester to go on having sexual relations with her by saying first that she was still in Chester's power,[2] a bondage resulting from thirty years of marriage and all its infinite ties and, finally, that she could not bring their relationship to an end by turning Chester out, "for I should know that I was committing a mean crime against something bigger than love" (*PG,* 301). The grace which imprisons Nina is the "something bigger than love," and whatever it is, it is something different from Cary's explanation.

It is one of the problems of *Prisoner of Grace* and of the trilogy that the reader cannot know with certainty just what it is that holds Nina in its iron grip and drives her steadily toward her destruction. Cary's assertion that Nina believed that Chester was "on the whole a good man" is contradicted in a number of passages. When Chester claims that Jim and Nina's child, born after he has married Nina, looks like him and pretends that the baby is his own, Nina characterizes the pretense as "ugly and dangerous" (*PG,* 17). Later, she is so repulsed by his behavior as a politician that she "would

feel a real hatred" against him and be terrified by the emotion (*PG,* 42).
When she can no longer stand him, she leaves Chester, but he compels her
to return to him and then she begins to hate him in earnest. In her anger
she attempts to kill herself by trying to jump from her bedroom window
(*PG,* 229). It is also true, however, that at various places in the novel Nina
defends Chester against criticism, even her own. Furthermore, *Prisoner of
Grace* is undertaken as a defense of a "great man."

The novel divides into the private story of a love triangle, involving
Nina, Chester, and Jim, and a public story, involving the political and
professional careers of Chester and Jim. The love story is unusual and
interesting. When Aunt Latter manipulates Nina, pregnant by Jim, into a
loveless marriage with Chester Nimmo, it is not only because it will
prevent the Latter name from being involved in a scandal but also because
she sees Nimmo as a rising power in the country and wants to see the Latter
family interests protected and advanced by his efforts.

Chester and Nina remain married for thirty years. In that time she tries
twice to kill herself, once with an overdose of sleeping pills and once by
attempting to jump to her death from her bedroom. She bears two
children, Tom and Sally, both fathered by Jim; and when, at the age of
forty-five she finally divorces Chester, she is again pregnant with one of
Jim's children. She marries Jim and hopes for happiness, but the arrival of
Chester at Palm Cottage, where she and Jim are living, brings that dream
to an end. She resumes sex with Chester and shortly thereafter tries again
to kill herself, this time by throwing herself under the wheels of a bus.
Within a short time of her recovery from this "accident," as she insists on
calling it, Jim kills her. Chester dies of a heart attack, and Jim is left to
hang.

Nina's personal story of divided loyalty and its tragic outcome is told
within her account of another series of events, those marking out the
public lives of Jim Latter and Chester Nimmo from the time of her
marriage to her resumption of sexual activity with her ex-husband. It is for
the purpose of telling this second story that Nina undertakes to write
Prisoner of Grace. In it she gives in outline form a sketch of Chester's
political career over a period of twenty-eight years. She also provides the
reader with glimpses of Jim's career as a colonial officer, working in Africa
with the Luga tribe, whose members Jim is fanatically determined to
shield from modernization.

Chester advances from the city council to the county council and from it
to the national government. Eventually he becomes a candidate for the
leadership of his party and the position of prime minister. The period

leading through World War I and into the General Strike of 1926 is seen as one of intense struggle. The story focuses on Chester's meteoric rise so that Cary can observe and describe the workings of political life. In particular, Cary raises the question of whether a politician, who must make his way by persuading large numbers of people to vote for him and the holders of great wealth to give their money to his party, can always be truthful.

The answer, obvious to Cary, is that he cannot. Cary compares the politician who must bend the truth for the nation's good with the mother who tells the child being taken to the dentist that he will suffer no pain. Having disposed of that issue, Cary goes on to the more important question, whether the politician is able to keep his principles.

I do not think the novel provides an answer to this question. Much of the novel is a dismal record of Chester's lying and deceiving, shifting sides, abandoning friends, and manipulating people and events for his political advantage. Very close to the end of the book, Nina says of Chester that he "was a man who had long ceased to know what did not suit him" (*PG*, 269). On the other hand, Nina says, truthfully enough, "It's no good, in fact, pretending that there is any easy way to solve political questions, because they are all so mixed up with feelings and prejudices that people have to be persuaded and induced to do and think rightly (unless you just shoot them, which is impossible in a democracy)" (*PG*, 158). Nina makes this defense of Chester in relation to the Bank Rams scandal, in which Chester had benefited while in office from shares in a company operating under a government contract.

The issue is, of course, whether Chester was dishonest in the matter, that is, whether he acted without principles. Cary does not give the reader enough information to answer this question. Clearly, Chester was prepared to go on profiting from the shares as long as there was no danger to him from so doing. It is equally true that he was a member of the government at the time. But, according to Nina, he had no specially advantageous information in hand when he made the share purchases, no more, that is, than any other man of business might have had. Chester, then, seems to stand clear of the charge of a breach of principles, of deliberate wrongdoing. The reader is not, however, altogether convinced by Nina's argument, and Chester walks away from the Bank Rams scandal smelling slightly of brimstone.

It is Chester's business to persuade people to support him and his party, to ward off attacks from his political opponents, and to attempt to translate into legislation as much of his party's program as possible. To accomplish any of these things, he must have a constituency. Several times in the course of the novel, Chester, in order to win such a constituency, completely reverses his position on a major issue. Before the outbreak of hostilities in 1914, Chester is a leading force in the Peace party, whose members oppose the war on moral and religious grounds. After the outbreak of fighting, he actually accepts a ministry in the wartime government. An abandonment of principles? Not at all in Chester's view, simply an adaptation to a new political reality. As long as war was only a possibility, a peace party had credibility. Once the fighting began, his only hope of retaining a sizeable constituency is to join the war party.

Although it is possible to make a continuing case for Chester throughout the novel, as Cary does in a letter to Andrew Wright, in which he writes, "What I believe is what Nimmo believes, that wangle is inevitable in the modern state, that is to say, there is no choice between persuading people and shooting them,"[3] it is not easy to make as good a case for Nina. There is a general concurrence among those who have written on the subject, with a strong demurrer from Barbara Fisher in her analysis of *Prisoner of Grace,* that Nina loses her way and strays into a moral swamp, unable, in the end, to make any choices. Indeed, her confusion and her despair are movingly expressed at the close of the novel when she states that she cannot throw Chester out of her house because she would "despise herself" and that to do so would "destroy my happiness and all the joy of my life, and Jim can only shoot me dead" (*PG,* 301).

Except The Lord

The second volume of Cary's trilogy appeared in 1953, a year after *A Prisoner of Grace.* The novel was written more swiftly than the first volume had been; Cary took time between the completion of *Prisoner of Grace* and *Except The Lord* to work on the short stories which he had begun to write again after a lapse of nearly thirty years. The second volume is Chester Nimmo's story, a memoir of his childhood and early manhood, all the action occurring before he meets Nina. It is a remarkable story, one that gives a powerful, unforgettable picture of the poverty-stricken Devon laborer's family life in the 1860s.

The novel brings Chester only to his twenty-fifth birthday, but it is written from the point of view of a man in his seventies, at the end of his political career and, as we come to know, close to the end of his life. The title, *Except The Lord,* comes from the opening verse of Chester's father's favorite psalm, which begins, "Except the Lord build the house, their labour is but lost that built it." Writing at the end of his life, Chester has

come to believe, or so he says, that he has been misled in thinking that
the idealism that has lain for a lifetime at the center of his activities can
be translated into the social fabric of the nation. And in *Except The Lord*
Chester does go from belief to loss of belief to despair and finally in the
closing passages of the book to hope and faith again.

All of the problems regarding the credibility of the narrator, which are
raised in *Prisoner of Grace,* are present in this second volume. To whom,
for example, is Chester addressing the story? To Nina, in order to cajole
her into sexual compliance? To the general public for the purpose of
executing yet another "wangle"? Or is it an honest record of the "making" of Chester Nimmo's soul? No completely satisfactory answer can be
given because Cary does not give the reader enough information. The
reader is left with a puzzle, a tissue of contradictions and moral riddles
for which there are no solutions.

It has been said elsewhere that Cary was extraordinarily good at
depicting the lives of children. In *Except The Lord* he surpasses himself.
The account of the lives of Chester and his brothers and sisters is vivid,
vital, and completely compelling. One is prepared to take an oath that
this is how poor children lived and suffered and dreamed their dreams in
the rural backwaters of Devon in the 1860s. Not even in Dickens is the
sense of deprivation, helplessness, and confusion resulting from such
suffering more powerfully conveyed. It is this part of the story that goes
so far toward establishing Chester as a sympathetic character. Whatever
Nina's and Jim's stories do to discredit Chester Nimmo as a man of
honor, the childhood sections of *Except The Lord* are always in the
balance, weighing in his behalf.

Chester's father is a small farmer and an evangelist preacher. When
the story opens there are five children: Richard, Georgina, Chester,
Ruth, and Dorothy, who soon dies of tuberculosis, contracted from the
mother, who is herself perishing of the disease. Chester's father is unable
to make a success of farming for the reason that he devotes too much time
to his preaching and because in his effort to emulate the life of Christ, he
gives his money away as fast as he makes it. When Chester is six years
old, his father loses their farm, Highfallow, and is compelled to move
into the village and take up the life of a farm laborer. Until Chester leaves
home, the action of the story centers on the home and the various
struggles of the members of the family to make their ways in a narrow,
hostile world.

Of the many compelling events which make up the first section of the
book, two are of particular importance in the shaping of Chester's life.

The first involves his sister Georgina's determination to go to work in the public house, following her mother's death and in defiance of her father's forbidding her to do so. The confrontation is of significance beyond its function in the plot of the novel. The father, who insists that to work in a public house puts Georgina's soul in danger and is service rendered the devil, takes the stand of the idealist, the true believer and the repudiator of moral compromise. Georgina's position is that the family cannot do without the money.

Georgina acts out of a kind of necessity. Prior to her decision to go to the public house, she had worked for G., the grocer. Although Cary does not allow it to be said straight out, it is clear that G. is demanding sexual favors from Georgina, who is, perhaps, twelve or thirteen years old at the time. Rumors begin to circulate in the village and are brought home to Georgina by Richard. They quarrel, and their father overhears enough to become suspicious. He asks Georgina what G. has been doing to her. She lies and says that nothing has happened. This lie is a great shock to her father, to Chester, who hears his sister speak it, and to Georgina, who goes deathly pale at its utterance.

Georgina's decision to go to the public house, then, is a political decision, choosing not the "right" course of action, which is not available to her, but the better of the two "bad" alternatives, which are open to her. Her decision to lie to her father is also a political as well as a moral decision. Aware of the consequences for herself, for her family, for G., and most especially for her father, she lies, to avert the disaster that would follow her telling her father the truth. Through her lie and by means of her decision to go to the public house to work, Georgina finds out how to manage her father, who is ill-suited to deal with the practical affairs of life. She becomes the effective head of the family and their secular guide. The father remains the spiritual head of the group, but his authority is diminished in their workaday lives. In the family crises precipitated by G., Georgina behaves as a politician. It is a lesson not lost on Chester, although he is too young at the time to fully understand what has happened.

The second event that leaves a permanent mark on Chester's life is his going to Lilmouth Great Fair and attending a performance of *Maria Marten*, a popular melodrama. For Chester's father and for all of his sect and dozens like it, the theater is a "temple of lies, where men and women practiced feigning as an art, to deceive and confuse honest souls—."[4] Chester had been expressly forbidden to enter a theater, but he defies his father's teachings and goes in to the theater tent, pressing forward until he is in the front row. To Chester's immense astonishment, he no sooner achieves his place at the ropes when he sees Georgina in another part of the crowd.

Cary takes pains to point out that the play, *Maria Marten,* which represents a virtuous village girl raped and later murdered by a dissolute squire's son, was based on a factual case. The actual events involved a young woman with several illegitimate children and a farmer's son, who has an affair with Maria and kills her when she attempts to blackmail him into marriage. Chester points out that at the time he saw the play, he had no idea of the real story. The drama he saw impressed itself on him as "a story of the cruelest kind of wrong inflicted by the rich upon the poor" (*EL,* 87). He wonders that the play and others like it, which were incredibly powerful, did not bring bloody revolution to England: "For its power was incredible. As I say, it was decisive in my life."

Not only does the play intensify that sense of class conflict of which Chester is already aware but it also makes him aware of the power of evil, or what he perceived then to be evil. The villain of the piece, Corder, comes forward at the end of the action to confess his guilt and to do it with defiance. Chester records that when Corder stood in front of him, delivering his soliloquies, Chester's heart almost failed him. And when the actor's eyes seemed to met his, "they sent forth an indescribable thrill—it seemed that something flashed from the very centre of evil into my deepest soul" (*EL,* 89). What the young Chester has recognized, without fully understanding it, is the power of the orator to sway his audience.

Chester makes a point of saying that the drama aroused in the audience the deepest emotions. Chester wept, people cried out in pain and anger. Some groaned aloud, and one young woman broke into hysterical sobs. He said they suffered more than if a genuine tragedy had befallen them. Later in life, Chester, as a politician playing on the emotions of his listeners, employs the strategy of *Maria Marten* to win the support of the voters. Beginning with sordid facts, he constructs a drama in which he and his party represent the forces of virtue and truth and his opponents, the army of sin and lies, and, playing upon the susceptibilities of the audience, moves them to pity and terror. This device is what Jim Latter calls "wangling."

The issue is central to Cary's subject. A modern democracy, Cary says, is governed by demagoguery. Fisher argues that Cary saw Chester Nimmo as one of the demagogues referred to in *Art And Reality,* whose power through speaking is so great that he feared that they threatened civilization.[5] She equates his work in the novel with the devil's and she sees a comparison between Chester and Hitler.[6] Bloom characterizes Chester as a man of "duplicity and ruthless calculation."[7]

Echeruo comes closer, however, to describing what is actually taking place and, as a consequence, approaches the central issue in the novel. He reminds us that the basic political point of the novel lies in the line, "Except the Lord build the house, their labour is but lost that built it." "The Psalm," he points out, "does not ask for the abandonment of all political action but for the recognition of its limitations."[8] Cary dramatizes throughout the trilogy the inability of political action to bring about order. Insofar as a democracy can be governed at all and any approach to order made, the task is achieved by such men as Chester Nimmo through the power of the spoken word. Cary has Jim Latter insist that "if a man or country gives up the truth, the absolute truth, they are throwing away the anchor and drifting slowly but surely to destruction."[9] Cary may have believed this or he may not, but his second trilogy tells us plainly that if we are to preserve political democracy, we must be prepared to surrender Jim Latter's ideal of honor as an unattainable dream.

Another aspect of *Except The Lord* is Chester's attitude toward women and the role of women in the early years of his life. He opens the story with a sentence of praise for three particular women, Georgina, Nina, and his mother, the trio being called "the three noblest" women he had known. This is neither flattery nor a conventional nod to the nineteenth-century ideal of woman's moral superiority. Midway through the novel, Chester interrupts his narrative to speak in general about women and about what he describes as their special knowledge.

Denying that he is espousing any "mystic doctrine" regarding women's superiority, he says that women are "concerned with a permanent truth, with problems of loyalty and responsibility that never change their essense . . . ," unlike men, who are forever engaged in the ephemeral concerns of politics (*EL,* 209). Fisher argues that Chester's praise of women is only a gaudy cloth thrown over the treachery of his own relations with women. "He has," she insists, "been willing to let these women suffer, and others like them in his drive to destroy our civilization." Worse than this, she finds him incapable of unselfish feeling. He goes to Georgina's grave and thinks of ways to make political use of Georgina. "He is incapable of wholly unselfish feeling. He must always turn everything to his own selfish advantage, and that, Cary would say, is the Devil."[10]

Fisher's indictment is harsh. Chester exploits Nina and, to a lesser degree Georgina, but the trilogy supports the argument that Chester also genuinely loves these two women and honors them for what he regards as their great and abiding virtues of loyalty and courage. Chester's selfishness, his inability to regard anyone completely unselfishly, is an important part of Cary's point that there is always an element of "wangle" in human relations, as there must be in politics.

Not Honour More

In the fall of 1953 Cary toured the United States. In November *Except The Lord* was published in England and the United States. With the appearance of the second volume of the trilogy, he began to work on *Not Honour More*.[11] But following his return to England he did not settle down to finish the novel. Instead, in the spring in 1954 he went on a lecture tour to Italy, in June and July he toured Germany and Berlin, and in the fall and early winter he lectured in France, Sweden, Finland, and Denmark.[12] The novel was not published until 1955.

Appropriately, the title of the novel is drawn from "To Lucasa, On Going to the Wars," a poem by the cavalier poet, Richard Lovelace, a champion of King Charles I and a defender of a lost dream. The title is a brilliant choice, summarizing Jim Latter's precept of the primacy of honor while, at the same time, reminding the reader of the possibly ironic attitudinizing in the poem itself. Jim Latter regards the poem as a supreme statement of his views regarding the virtuous ideal, a literary judgment which reveals the idiosyncratic quality of his mind as well as its dangerous limitations.

Like Nina, Jim is an orphan, not from the death of his parents but because of his separation from them. In their childhood and early youth, Jim and Nina are often together and Aunt Latter always told Nina to do the things Jim wants to do and to do them cheerfully. He is Aunt Latter's favorite nephew. Jim grows up both spoiled and deprived. Lonely, intense, physically brave but sometimes driven by his demons to take dangerous risks with his sailboat that threaten to drown both himself and Nina, he is stubborn, irascible, and domineering. He alternately makes Nina bountifully happy and equally miserable with his demands and moods.

Shortly after entering a regiment, he gets Nina pregnant and rather than lose his place by marrying, he allows Aunt Latter to make up a match between the girl he is supposed to love and Chester Nimmo. Later, when he returns on a leave, he berates Nina for having married Chester and reasserts his right to have sex with her on the grounds that they love one another, a condition which takes precedence over the commitment of her marriage vows. Nina offers him little resistance. She does love him.

As the Jim Latter story is developed in *Prisoner of Grace* and *Not Honour More,* Jim is shown to have three obsessions—Nina, the Lugas, and Chester Nimmo. Jim regards Nina as belonging to him, the fact of his having abandoned her to Aunt Latter's devices and allowed her to be married to Chester being no deterrent to his claim. The Lugas are an African tribe with whom he works during his African years. His perception of them as nature's gentlemen enables him to persuade himself that they can only be protected from corruption by being kept free from modernization. He ruins himself financially and loses credibility with them and the general public by the violence of his views. Chester Nimmo becomes the arch fiend in Jim's mythology of modern life, the man who is bent on destroying civilization. Jim never understands that he hates Chester because Chester is married to Nina and because he is an effective leader of men, whereas Jim is not.

The events of the novel cover a relatively brief period of the General Strike from about 1 May 1926 to his imprisonment for murdering Nina. The occasion of the narrative is Jim's failure to convince the press that he has committed the crime to save England from wangling. His story, dictated to a police secretary while waiting trial and expecting to be hanged, is his defense against the charge made in the papers that he killed Nina for taking money and jewelry from Chester and sleeping with him. He comes to the end of the book convinced that he has executed Nina as "an example." But in fact he is quite mad, at least so wildly deluded as to be acting like a madman.

Jim's story is filled with barely controlled rage and confusion. At the outset of the story, he is married to Nina, who has lately left Chester. Coming home to Palm Cottage unexpectedly, he finds Chester "interfering" with his wife. He takes out his twenty-two caliber rifle and fires three shots at Chester in an attempt to kill him. Chester, over seventy years of age, manages to save himself by making a back somersault through a ground floor window. He subsequently denies that Jim has attacked him; and Jim, attempting to persuade the press to print his charge that Chester has made improper advances to his wife, finds that no paper will print such a statement for fear of libel.

These private struggles involving Jim, Nina, and Chester are acted against the potentially violent backdrop of the General Strike, which Jim regards as a test of the nation's backbone and willingness to stand up to the "Bolshies," while Chester sees it as a heaven-sent opportunity for him to recapture a constituency and have himself voted back into office. He immediately forms a committee, designed to play a mediating role between the various elements in contention over the strike, and manages to have himself elected its chairman.

The town of Tarbiton, where the action of the novel is concentrated, has a fascist element, headed by a man named Brightman, and a communist group, led by Pincomb. Each of these groups maneuvers to benefit as much as possible from the social unrest caused by the disruption of transportation and so on in the country. The danger of violence is so great that the police cannot provide adequate protection, and a group called the Specials are formed to act as a kind of National Guard. Seeing an opportunity to silence opposition to his leadership and give a nuisance something to do, Chester manages to persuade Jim to take over the leadership of this group of quasi-police.

One of Jim's subordinates on the Specials, a man named Maufe, becomes engaged in a struggle with Pincomb during some street trouble. In attempting to arrest him, Maufe knocks Pincomb down. Pincomb suffers a fractured skull, and Maufe is charged with assault. In the ensuing trial, Chester and Nina withhold important information that might have saved Maufe from conviction. Maufe is convicted and sent to prison. His family is broken up, and, at least in Jim's view, a terrible injustice has been done.

Cary makes certain that the reader cannot know whether or not the information withheld by Chester with Nina's connivance would have been sufficient to get Maufe off the charge nor, in fact, whether Maufe is actually guilty or innocent of assault. Jim is absolutely certain that Maufe has been sacrificed by an ungrateful system. When he discovers from letters exchanged between Chester and his wife that Nina did not give full testimony during the Maufe trial, he determines to kill both Chester and Nina. Chester escapes, to die of a heart attack, but Nina is murdered.

Echeruo refers to the "furious pessimism" of *Not Honour More,* indeed, of the entire trilogy. This pessimism, he believes, is generated by the melancholy conclusion which Cary had reached before framing the trilogy, a philosophy of measured despair that finds the ideal of truth, honor, and justice in the public life of modern states an impossible dream. The assumption that life is fundamentally unfair is present in Cary's work from *The African Witch* onward. Gulley Jimson frequently alludes to it as do other of Cary's characters. But nowhere in his fiction is the lesson more thoroughly presented than in the political trilogy.

Fisher characterizes Chester as a liar, exploiter, traitor, and despot.[13] She makes him out to be the villain of the novels, but she is wrong. The trilogy has no villains as it has no heroes. Jim Latter is either mad or an utter fool. He is certainly no hero. Nina is not evil. The worst that can be said about her is that she is weak, that she likes comfort and dislikes unpleasantness. Chester is a man of driving ambition, who, at varying times in his life, is motivated to act by laudable principles. It can be argued that time corrupts him. Perhaps it does. Certainly his aggressive and faintly repulsive sexuality in the last years of his life suggest something unpleasant at work in him.

As powerful as the three stories are, they are weakened in their final effect by three failures. Cary provides no sustaining moral center by which the various events of the novel can be judged, and no character can be said to embody a set of values that lead the reader to envision a society or set of human relationships that make life endurable. Finally, whether intended or not, the reader is left with the feeling that no matter how wrong he is, Jim Latter is right.

His anger is the most convincing emotion in the three novels, and, inevitably, the reader will respond to that anger with some degree of sympathy. Although Cary carefully constructs Jim's story in such a way that the reader cannot intellectually agree with Jim's evaluation of the problems facing him and his country, he builds sympathy for Jim into the story in a way that cannot be missed. It is, I think, a further indication of failure in the trilogy that when Nina and Chester die, the reader feels little shock or grief. Compared with Jim's self-righteous anger, even their lives seem unimportant.

Chapter Eight
The Captive and the Free

Andrew Wright tells of having found in Cary's attic, "among many tantalizing boxes of fragments" of work in progress, "large chunks of a projected trilogy titled 'The Captive And The Free.'" According to Wright this abandoned trilogy was to have concerned itself "with the economic background of the 'twenties and 'thirties."[1] In the editor's note which serves as a postscript to *The Captive and the Free*, Winifred Davin writes that Cary had made three attempts to write a novel with this title. And it is almost certain that prior to the onset of his illness, he had intended a trilogy with a religious theme, of which one volume was to have been titled *The Captive and the Free*.

Cary's illness forced him to compromise on a single volume. For the last three years of his life he worked on the novel, abandoning it only in the final three months before his death in order to complete *Art and Reality*.[2] From the mass of manuscript material left by Cary and the many discussions the two women had held with him about the novel, Winifred Davin and Edith Millen pieced together the manuscript and saw it through to publication. The resulting book cannot be considered a finished work. There are internal inconsistencies of plot and chronology that Davin could not resolve. And, of course, Cary never regarded a book finished until he had cut, added, and revised extensively. Nevertheless, *The Captive and the Free* is an important novel. The reading public owes Davin and Millen a debt of gratitude.

Critical opinions regarding the quality of the novel vary widely. Golden Larsen, conceding that the novel has "some good writing in it and a few passages with genuine power," assigns the book to a minor place among Cary's novels.[3] Robert Bloom regards the book as essentially incomplete, not having "undergone the extensive final revision to which all of his novels were subjected. . . ." In contrast, David Cecil, writing in the introduction to the novel, asserts that it is one of Cary's "most important and memorable books."

The Captive and the Free is certainly important but probably not as a novel. Its value lies in the way in which it reveals Cary's attitude toward the fundamental issues of faith and belief. Insofar as it can be said that any character in the novels speaks for Cary, that character is Syson, the Church of England rector who loses his faith and lives to recover it on his way to prison. Although Syson is certainly no mouthpiece for the author, he probably is a vehicle for expressing certain ideas that Cary saw as central to the human condition, the most important of which is what Syson in his rebirth of faith calls "the miracle of God's love in the world" (C, 326).

Early in his life, Cary found himself no longer capable of belief as defined by the thirty-nine articles of the Anglican church. Later, sometime in the late 1920s, following a very long period of reading and thinking extending over several years, Cary rediscovered his faith, not in the church but in a transcendence, the reality of which is made evident in man's sense of beauty and his capacity of love.

Characters

The polarity of the novel is established by four of Cary's characters: Preedy, the faith healer; Syson, the Anglican rector; Hooper, the opportunistic journalist; and Lord Tinney, the atheistic rationalist.[4] Preedy is the most difficult to comprehend. The problem is due, primarily, to Cary's refusal to clarify his own position regarding Preedy, who is represented in the novel as a possibly mad but certainly obsessed man, responsible for the deaths of several people, among them two children, both of whom would have lived had they been allowed conventional medical treatment. Within the immediate action of the novel, two persons are placed under Preedy's hands for treatment. One, a wealthy young woman crippled in a riding accident, and the other a young girl suffering from tuberculosis. The young woman is cured of her paralysis. The child dies. Cary gives the reader an even score.

More troubling than this ambiguity is his handling of Preedy himself. While in his twenties, Preedy seduces a fourteen-year-old girl named Alice Rodker. She becomes pregnant by him. He refuses to marry her, and because she will not tell the police who fathered the child, she is sent away for two years to a remand home. While she is in the home, Preedy undergoes a religious conversion in which he sees Alice as God's instrument in his redemption. Once she is out of the home, he seeks her out. When her child falls ill with meningitis, Preedy will not allow her to take it to a doctor. He insists that if she will only believe, the child will be cured. The child dies. Alice leaves Preedy, who insists that the child's death was due to her stubbornness in refusing to believe in God.

Others who come to the Pants Road Mission, where Preedy practices his faith cures, are sometimes healed, sometimes not. Alice Rodker, who throughout the novel is involved in an intense hate-love relationship with Preedy, believes that Preedy is mad. She never doubts his sincerity but feels that children must be protected from him. She regards him as a murderer. Syson believes that Preedy's god is a devil. Hooper sees him as good copy, and Tinney can find no rational place for a Preedy in his view of reality.

What Cary thinks about Preedy is not any clearer than is what Cary thinks about Gulley Jimson or Aissa or Chester Nimmo. Bloom puts the problem very well in his discussion of *The Captive and the Free:* "Since it is a book which occupied Cary during the last months of his life, which he wanted desperately to finish before he died, and which treats of matters of the highest importance to him, it would seem that he was at last ready to make the kind of assessment of the experience of his characters which he had, in one way or another, been avoiding for almost thirty years."[5]

But, as Bloom goes on to point out, Cary does nothing of the sort. Preedy remains thoroughly ambiguous. In a kind of despairing comment, Bloom writes, "Perhaps, in the end, only energy and intensity are real for Cary."[6] In the case of *The Captive and the Free,* it is of course possible that upon rewriting and revising, Cary would have brought Preedy and the others into focus; it is possible but unlikely.

The issue is not really one of what Bloom calls energy and intensity. To bring Preedy into the absolute relationship with the events in which he is involved would have compelled Cary to construct a moral universe in which good and evil are defined. That Cary resolutely refused to do. The poles of reference in *The Captive and the Free,* as Foster points out, are characters who represent four expressions of or attitudes toward religion. Otherwise stated, truth is unattainable. Only alternatives of action are available to the Cary character.

The point can be illustrated by looking at the ways in which Preedy is presented. We are told, and Preedy freely confesses, that he was a vicious young wastrel, a seducer, a man without meaning, who has become obsessed with God. In describing this conversion and its consequences, Cary says, "Preedy has been taken to pieces by experts. They say, 'The typical schizoid—a little Hitler. You find him everywhere—the village boy who goes from Mass to do murder is the basic type. And it works

both ways. Sudden conversions are nearly all schizoid—St. Augustine,
St. Francis, all the young men who commit every kind of crime or folly,
even extreme cruelties, and then suddenly turn to religion, where they
are equally violent and equally indifferent to authority, prudence, or
common sense'" (*C,* 53).

Cary, however, creates two events that seem to contradict the experts,
one of which occurs before the action of the story commences and the
other, toward the end of the novel. The first recounts Preedy's conversion
at the feet of the evangelist, Jackson, who, preaching on Hyde Park
Corner, brings Preedy to God. The second action is more powerful and
compelling in justifying Preedy's conduct. In an intensely dramatic
moment when Ada Rollwright's father is struggling to convince his wife
that the girl must be allowed to see a doctor, and the mother is striving to
prevent that from happening, Preedy leaves the family to fight it out and
goes for a walk beside the sea.

A medical doctor, called by the father to examine the child, comes
down onto the beach and speaks Ada Rollwright's name. The sound of
the name breaks through Preedy's gloomy reflections:

He was suddenly in a different world; the walls had gone and the darkness was no
longer an enclosed, stifling dark of the grave, but an enormous night in which
darkness was not the absence of light but the presence of things unseen—of a
whole world of being not known or realized before. He stook looking out to the
sea. . . . But he saw it only with his eyes, without recognition. All his senses
were turned inwards; he was gazing into this immensity of his vision, straining
his eyes to distinguish some form, listening for an intelligent sound. (*C,* 297)

The forms take shape in Preedy's mind. He has a vision of God
presiding over the fiery images of Preedy's childhood, of Old Testament
stories, "soaked in treachery and blood," of the testing of Abraham and
Isaac's deliverance. Preedy emerges from the absorption in his vision
sufficiently to ask if this world today is "any different from the one of the
Old Testament"? By implication, it is not. Man is still a hater of truth,
malicious, lustful, and mean.

Preedy then concludes, and here the voice sounds as if it is, at least in
part, Cary's own. "The miracle of history was that any goodness, any
truth, had ever appeared on earth—how, in this everlasting war between
the few good and the enormous mass of evil, the smallest remnant of the
faithful survived." How did they . . . maintain their faith? "By revelation only. By the sudden showing forth of his power, his grandeur, by

the word out of the air, the voice heard at night in the sleepy soul unguarded and released from selfish fear, by the touch of kindness, the glance of a passer-by in the street, the mere glimpse of a face made beautiful by a momentary affection" (C, 298).

This last passage goes far, in my estimation, to explain Cary's refusal to structure his own books in such a way as to embody a morally coherent universe. The world, as Cary saw it, is without moral coherence. And the presence of God in it is known not through the scriptures or the religions they express but through revelation only. This revelation is sporadic, fleeting, blinding in its intensity but useless as a moral guide. It comes to the Preedys of the world as often as to the Sysons and may be used by both, for good or evil.

Only three people in the novel are truly free when the novel ends— Preedy, who has had his second and most powerful vision; Alice Rodker, who has, in her words, "got straight again" and can take anything; and Syson, on his way to prison but having recovered his faith, which will enable him to write a book about his experience. In a sense, Cary has identified himself with all three of these characters, saints and sinners alike. He remains true to his convictions and leaves his moral position ambiguous to the very end.

The Plot

The story is simple enough. As curate of St. Enoch's parish, Syson is confronted with the problem of dealing with the Pants Road Mission and Preedy's faith healing. He foolishly makes statements condemning Preedy and finds himself charged with libel. During the trial he finds that he is unable to affirm that he absolutely believes in the ability of God to perform miracles of healing and is soon led to admit that he does not believe literally in the articles of the church. He loses his case and is fined heavily. The revelation of his own disbelief has a profound effect on Syson. He leaves the church and his wife and children, determined to find the truth of what he does believe and to expose Preedy for the exploiter and devil worshipper he believes him to be.

Syson fades temporarily from the action to make way for Joanna Rideout and Harry Hooper. Joanna is the daughter of Lady Rideout, an old woman dying of cancer, who has a position of power on the board of directors of the Argus, a staid, old-fashioned newspaper facing declining fortunes. Hooper is a journalist-editor on the Argus who wants to modernize the paper. He sees Preedy and the Pants Road Mission as just the sort of lurid material that will pull in readers. He seduces Joanna with the vague idea of gaining influence on the board of directors through Lady Rideout's daughter.

Alice Rodker, seduced by Preedy at fourteen, comes into the story when she is called as a witness for the defense in Syson's trial. Furious at being dragged into notoriety again, she lies about her relationship with Preedy, insisting that she has no idea who the actual father of her child was, that she was very promiscuous at the time of its conception. She turns to Joanna for help when she once again finds herself being sought by Preedy. But in the end she returns to care for Preedy, having undergone some sort of religious experience that rids her of her bitterness and anger and enables her to live a life of spiritual and emotional freedom.

Lady Rideout dies, Hooper and Joanna marry, Syson goes to prison, and the *Argus* goes into the hands of a northern industrialist who wishes to combine a northern daily with a London paper. It is an important part of the story that Joanna and Hooper do not make any spiritual progress whatever. Perhaps Hooper does lose a degree of his selfishness through the course of the story. At least he decides to marry Joanna after first telling her that, if she decides to have the child, it is entirely her affair and nothing to do with him. He offers abortion money, which Joanna declines to accept. But Joanna ends as she begins.

The obvious points of interest in the novel are Alice Rodker, Preedy, and Syson. As is usual in Cary's fictions, there is a considerable amount of violence involving the chief characters. Alice is humiliated by Preedy, bitten by a dog, terrorized by the police, and locked away in a remand home for two years, all as a result of her sexual infatuation with Preedy. At the end of the novel, Preedy strikes her in the face, bloodying her nose and swelling her cheek until her left eye almost vanishes. She accepts this abuse and determines to stay on.

Syson becomes involved in various skirmishes with the police and with Preedy as he passes out libelous leaflets outside the Pants Road Mission. When he is arrested a second time and is being hurried out of the court house under police protection on his way to jail, one of Preedy's followers throws a bottle that strikes him on the forehead. Before his arrest he is brutally indifferent to his wife and to her efforts to bring him back to his "senses" by persuading him to come to her family's home for a long rest.

The damage done to women in the story is quite extensive. Ada Rollwright dies of tuberculosis. Alice Rodker's life is darkened by her early involvement with Preedy. She loses her child through his fanaticism. Lady Rideout dies. Joanna marries a man whose arrogance and selfishness seem certain guarantees of her future suffering.

It is, however, only fair to say that Barbara Fisher sees the novel as a final justification of women. In her view of the work, "what Cary called the creative imagination is shown working through the women of this novel, to make theirs the first generation in our society to have recognized freedom as responsibility, and to have chosen that role for themselves."[7] She sees Alice Rodker's refusal to answer at the trial as suggestive of Christ's silence at His trial "and more particularly to suggest how Mary, His mother, might have answered, in the same circumstances." Fisher suggests that the "women of this novel contrast with those in Cary's previous novels, and have, as it were, his farewell blessing."[8] The reader is likely to remain unconvinced, seeing more of the blow than the blessing in Cary's final gesture.

Chapter Nine

The Short Stories

Cary had two intense periods of short-story writing, one at the beginning, the other at the end of his career. While serving in Nigeria he wrote many stories, most of which he destroyed. By the time of his return from Africa in December 1919, he had sold three stories to the *Saturday Evening Post* and carried several more home with him on the ship. These he worked on during the passage to England and sold a few months later to the *Post*. Twenty-five years later he returned to the short story and wrote the bulk of those which were later collected and published under the title of *Spring Song*, first published in 1951 and expanded in subsequent publications.

Originally, Cary began writing short stories with the hope of creating a source of income that might allow him to leave the Nigerian Service and return to England permanently. He had no idea of treating these stories as serious literature. In fact, he referred to them as pot boilers. When the *Post* began accepting his stories in 1920, he published them under the name Thomas Joyce, in order to reserve the name Joyce Cary for the serious work he planned in his novels.

The *Post* stories are certainly slight. Set in France and drawn freely from Cary's youthful experiences there, they are formula fiction, made up, as Cary wrote in a letter from Nigeria to his wife, of "a little sentiment. A little incident, and a surprise."[1] Between 31 January and 9 October 1920 the *Post* published ten of Cary's stories, finding in them just the qualities of slickness and sentiment that appealed to its readers. By the end of the summer, Cary felt that his financial future was secure. But in October the magazine returned a batch of his stories with the complaint that they were too literary.[2] Cary was never able to sell them another of his stories.

That Cary should have so abruptly lost his ability to write saleable stories is puzzling. In fact, it raises questions that can, in all probability, never be adequately answered. The possibility exists, however, that Cary deliberately scuttled his treasure ship.

Cary seems to have had in his early adult life an absolute revulsion against succeeding. He threw up his painting after working hard to develop some skill and understanding of the profession. He entered Oxford, neglected his work, and, although possessed of a fine intelligence, took a fourth in his examinations, a failure too profound to be credible. Following the Oxford disaster, he fled to Montenegro, where he nearly succeeded in getting himself killed. He then entered the Nigerian Service, consigning himself to a self-imposed purgatory, involving extreme physical discomfort, professional obscurity, and separation from his wife, whom he had pursued only to abandon.

He had no sooner entered the Nigerian Service than he began struggling desperately to get out of it. Returning to England in 1919 with the promise of success and financial independence in his hands, he had, within nine months, lost the ability to write a saleable story. It was to be another ten years before he managed to bring a novel to completion and offer it to a publisher. Surely, a history of failure of this magnitude in a man of Joyce Cary's physical and intellectual power suggests something other than ill luck. Discounting the possibility that some sinister Hardian fatality had singled Cary out for suffering, one is left with the suspicion that Cary was deliberately failing.

After the *Post* stopped buying his stories, Cary sold an occasional story to the *Strand Magazine* and *Hutchinson's,* but these sales number only five and in 1923 ceased altogether. World War II stirred memories in Cary of his service during the Great War in the Cameroons, and in 1945 he wrote and sold to *Windmill* magazine a heavily autobiographical story of his war experience, titled "Bush River."[3] He was soon writing stories again and continued to write them until his death, several of them being published posthumously.

Wright has pointed out that the later stories, beginning with "Bush River," divide roughly into three groups: stories of Africa, old age, and childhood. He finds that they illustrate "in simpler focus the themes of the novels. . . ."[4] He also considers them "interesting and important in their own right." The stories of old age contain echoes of the stories of Katherine Mansfield, especially stories such as "Miss Brill." The African stories are interesting for the picture they give the reader of Cary's life in Nigeria and the Cameroons. But the stories of childhood seem to have the most life and vitality. These stories of discovery, as Wright calls them, are brimming with energy.

One of the best is the title story of the collection, "Spring Song." It is not really a story at all but a lightning glance at a minor episode in the life of elder sister Gladys, condemned by an indifferent fate to walk her very much smaller brother and sister in the park on an early spring day. Gladys would much rather be walking alone, perhaps to be spoken to by the soldiers strolling in the park. Although she may not be quite old enough for that sort of romantic excitement, she is old enough to resent the job of being a nurse.

Maggie, the little girl, is pushing a doll's baby carriage with a missing wheel and, in a loud voice, telling a story that is filled with nonsense words. Gladys makes futile attempts to make Maggie tell her story in conventional words, but the child insists on retaining her "akkerpeetie" man who owns a "pootle," a creature from "Baffrica."

Suddenly the child stops telling her story and demands of her five-year-old brother, "Tom, Tom, did you believe my story?" Tom says that he did, arousing Gladys's wrath, who accuses him of not having listened to the story. Compelled by Gladys to admit that he does not know what the story means, he insists on liking it. Then the two little children begin to dance around in delight, shouting, "An akkerpeetie man—and he had—a toople too."

Gladys rushes at the children, pulls them apart, and cries, "Stop that, you hear. I won't have it." Cary observes that she appeared to be frightened. Of course, the children stop their shouting and dancing. The boy goes back to examining his new shorts with their ample pockets and the little girl picks up her doll from the ground, where it had fallen and says to it, in the closing line of the story, as she places it in the doll carriage, "Lie down, Vera, or I'll give you such a smack on your poly."

The story is a small masterpiece. The moment, crumpled somewhat in the retelling, is caught perfectly, with wonderful humor and perception. The children are totally convincing. Gladys's confusion and anger, possibly even fear, in the face of the children's wild insistence on the "akkerpeetie" man, are entirely right. Even Maggie's warning to her doll is a triumph, not only for Maggie's imagination but for Cary's sense of his story as well.

Another story in the collection, "Growing Up," deals with children and their explosive imagination, but in an altogether different and, possibly, more alarming way. The children in "Growing Up" are two sisters, aged twelve and thirteen, who are in the garden, a wild, unkept piece of ground, "a bit of wild country," as the father describes it when he comes into it, looking for his daughters.

Jenny is lying on her stomach reading and Kate is daydreaming in the swing. They ignore their father's entrance into the garden and, lost in their own pursuits, barely say hello. Mr. Quick, the father, settles into a lawn chair to read the paper and soak up the sunshine. The quiet is disturbed by the arrival of the family dog, who attempts to tease Jenny into playing with her. Finally exasperated, Jenny hurls a piece of bamboo at the dog. Kate leaps up, shouting "Tiger, tiger," and the girls are off in mad pursuit of their pet, hurling sticks and pebbles and leaves after the fleeing animal.

Alarmed by the ferocity of the girl's assault on the dog, Mr. Quick struggles to extricate himself from his chair and go to the dog's rescue, shouting at the girls to stop. They suddenly turn on him, pummelling him, choking him, and tumbling over him until all three come crashing to the ground in the collapsed chair. The dog, overexcited by these events, flings herself on her master and bites his hand.

In a mercurial about face, the girls are suddenly overwhelmed with solicitude. They bring soap and water, wash the wound, and behave like stern nurses. Half amused and half perplexed by these goings-on, Mr. Quick concludes that his daughters are growing up and will soon not need him at all, except to pay the bills. Although he puts a brave front on matters, he is clearly troubled by this sudden sense of his swiftly passing life. Because his wife is busy with committee work, he decides to go to the club, but before he can leave, Jenny catches up with him and insists on looking once again at his hand. Father and daughter exchange a deep look, and Jenny runs back to the house. Mr. Quick decides that he too is growing up.

Wright makes the point that Cary's children's stories are all tales of discovery. "Growing Up" certainly is, but it is Mr. Quick who makes the discovery that his life is running away like water on a slope. Jenny and Kate do not really discover anything, except, perhaps, the intensity of their emotions. In contrast, Mr. Quick learns that he is increasingly on the fringes of his wife's and his children's lives. For the reader there is also the discovery that Mr. Quick is not going to do anything about his growing isolation except embrace it. "Growing Up" is an oddly disturbing story with some dark overtones.

As for the African stories, although praise is usually directed at "Bush River" and "Umaru," both of which deal with events in the war against the Germans in the Cameroons, the story "Buying A Horse" has a more general appeal and reflects a mingling of humor and humanity that the other African stories lack. It is a story about style, its quality and gaiety, and despite its African setting, it is primarily an Irish story.

Young Corner, the protagonist of "Buying A Horse," comes upon some army horses that have been lost during an engagement with the Germans in which the British forces have been forced to flee. One of the horses, a black Arab, is so weak that it is tottering on its legs, but it nibbles Corner's shirt and wins the young officer's heart. Although the horse is so weak that it is likely to die at any moment, Corner spares the animal and sets about discovering who owns it.

The owner of the horse turns out to be a Highlander, Major McA., who, learning that his pony, Satan, is alive and that Corner wants to buy him, gets up from his hospital bed, where he is recovering from gunshot wounds, and has himself conveyed by litter to the place where the horse is being kept. There, playing the part of the hero and skilled horse coper, he makes a comic effort to convince Corner that Satan is a wonderful horse and that it will break his heart to part with him. Corner eventually buys the horse for thirty shillings. McA. departs with an appeal to Corner to care for the horse well and asks for payment in cash.

"Success Story" is as painful as "Buying A Horse" is pleasant. The brief tale concerns an old man who sits down on a bench in the park; a child comes along, climbs into his lap and begins to jump up and down. The old man is unable to deal with the child. Then another child, the boy's sister, arrives and drags her brother off the old man. The old man is completely exhausted by the experience and must sit for some time until he struggles to his feet, gains his balance, and totters away, wearing a look of triumph.

Obviously, the man is very near the end of his life, his vitality almost spent. But he still struggles out into the park to take his exercise, although the encounter with the child demonstrates how weak he has become. There is something pathetic, pitiful about the old man. There is also a sense that the old man is something of another kind from the reader, not merely an older version of him.

Cary's achievement in the story, aside from the obvious one of depicting a very old and weak person suddenly confronted with the fierce vitality of a child, seems to be to strip away from his protagonist any qualities that will allow the reader to connect with him. The old man is presented as an alien figure, and the reader is left with the feeling that extreme age is itself an alienating condition. The black humor resulting from the old man's terror and discomfiture and the ludicrousness of his sense of achievement at being able to get up unaided from the park bench, adds to the subtle horror of the story.

The emphasis on flux that is a major element in Cary's fiction is overwhelmingly present in these short stories. One reads them with a feeling of the sliding quality of existence, of the ephemeral nature of all experience. Even the structure of the stories, which is generally that of a slice-of-life tale, adds to the sense of flow. The reader looks in on an action which began before Cary drew back the curtain and which continues after he lets it fall.

The stories convey no new message. They repeat the insistent refrain of the longer work—the new is created out of the destruction of the old. Life is a running fire that consumes its substance and roars on. Once this message is read in Cary's prose, one hears it like a drumbeat, thudding dominantly and irresistibly behind the music of events, characters, and setting.

Chapter Ten
The Critic and Journalist

A glance at the bibliography will show that Cary wrote a considerable amount of material about literature and about the creative process. In addition to the essays, Cary wrote a book entitled *Art and Reality,* devoted to the subject of artistic vision. This book, the prefaces he wrote for his novels, and his collected and uncollected essays, written for a variety of newspapers and magazines or delivered as lectures, constitute the body of his critical writing.

Although Cary was not a systematic critic and admitted that he had very little understanding of formal aesthetic theory, he was, nevertheless, remarkably well prepared to write about the fundamental nature of art. Not only was he a writer of fiction, he was a trained artist as well, and possessed a compendious knowledge of nineteenth- and twentieth-century painting.

In addition, Cary had spent the years from his joining the Nigerian Service to the publication of *Aissa Saved* immersing himself in English and European novels. Between 1920 and 1930 he spent a very considerable portion of his time reading. By the end of that ten-year period he had come to know in remarkable detail the work of all the major British and European writers of the nineteenth and twentieth centuries. In addition to the novelists, he had studied the work of philosophers and critics. There is no doubt that he was one of the most widely read writers of his or any other age.

Art and Reality

Rebecca West once observed that all literature worthy of the name is an expression of the search for salvation. To say this more simply still, all literature is about the struggle between life and death. Must a writer, to be considered a serious artist, provide readers with a definitive statement about the nature of this struggle? The answer is, probably, yes, it being difficult to imagine any fictive world in which the conflict does not underlie the action.

Cary certainly deals with the issues of life and death in his novels. They present a continuously unfolding drama of the struggle between the forces of life and the forces of destruction. What his novels do not do, however, is represent the creative forces and the destructive forces in clearly separated characters. It is not possible, for example, to say whether Chester Nimmo is a good man or an evil one. This being so, it is not possible to say whether life or death, good or evil, triumphs in the political trilogy.

Is the moral ambiguity that marks Cary's work a weakness in his fiction? Bloom certainly believes that it is, but before coming to any conclusion about the degree of Cary's failure, or even to say that he has failed at all, it is necessary to look carefully at the long essay entitled *Art and Reality*.

In *Art and Reality* Cary reveals what he considers to be the form and function of art, what it is and how it works. The essay is the key to his fiction and to understanding why he gives the impression of being an indeterminate writer, to employ Bloom's term, and why the question whether Chester Nimmo is a good or bad man is for him unanswerable.

Cary came to write *Art and Reality* only after answering finally for himself the question of the nature of ultimate reality. This mission of truth underlies not only the essay but all of his fiction as well, indeed, everything he published after 1930. What Cary is driving at in *Art and Reality* cannot be fully understood without keeping in mind his perception of reality.

Cary begins the essay with the assertion that the writer, if he is to write at all, must find some meaning in life. It is this meaning to which he is referring when he says that all great art has a meaning beyond itself.[1] Cary had, of course, found such a meaning or shape to existence. This meaning leads him to assert that no one can know what truth is, that it will always be only one person's picture of it (*AR*, 13). But it also leads him to the significant conclusion that "the most important part of man's existence . . . lies entirely within the domain of personal feeling" (*AR*, 24).

The two conclusions are not contradictory, at least not for Cary. He is convinced that men share common feelings. In fact, he goes so far as to say that "at a certain primitive level, all men agree" (*AR*, 153). What they agree about is "a common good in morality" and the values of courage, duty, affection, loyalty, self-discipline, and truth. That is to say, they agree in their feelings and only disagree at another level, such as the relative importance of the stated values.

Emerging in the essay is the picture of the artist, in touch with reality through the agency of his intuition, in touch with his fellowmen through the commonality of human feeling but cut off in his mind because of what Cary calls the gap between intuition and expression, itself only "another representative of the mind-body gap" (*AR*, 28). This gap, he insists, also exists between reality and our knowledge of it. Intuition puts us in touch with this reality but expression of it is always imperfect. The expression is, of course, the work of art and the intuition the source of the work.

Cary is convinced that the novelist is condemned to a certain kind of failure in the practice of his art, for the reason that the novel is invariably only a partial view of things. This limited vision is a product of the artist's confinement within the boundaries of his own limited vision and the limitation of the novel itself. By a frustrating paradox, the more comprehensive a novel becomes in scope, the more it loses power and significance. It is Cary's judgment that the novel will invariably weaken in force as it expands in scope. The hope, therefore, of constructing a novel both sufficiently broad in scope and concentrated in focus to give a complete picture of the truth is a fool's dream.

The reader can begin to see where Cary's argument is inevitably leading him, and if we consider Cary's attitude toward allegory, the direction will become even more clear. To put it too simply, Cary regards allegory as a form of lying, particularly when the writer begins to handle his characters as allegorical figures. The powerful example he draws on to make his point is taken from Hardy's *Tess of the D'Urbervilles.* Toward the end of that novel, Tess is fleeing across Salisbury Plains, lost in the fog, vainly striving to escape from the police. Exhausted, she seeks a dry place to lie down on. The fog lifts. The reader sees that Tess is lying on one of the monoliths in Stonehenge, and Hardy calls the stone a stone of sacrifice.

Cary is shocked and deeply offended by what Hardy does with Tess (*AR*, 168). He calls the scene "disastrous," because Hardy has not allowed Tess to remain Tess but turned her into an allegorical figure of meaning. In Cary's words, she has "become a figment, a stage property." Cary wanted her to remain Tess, caught in her personal tragedy, a wholly differentiated character whose meaning is herself. What he most emphatically does not want is for Hardy to convert Tess into a stated meaning. In Cary's view of reality and, in light of that, of art, Hardy lies

when he converts Tess into a figure of sacrifice. He breaks the vessel of his
art and spills out of it all its virtue, that is, the partial truth he had so
effectively gathered in the development of Tess as a character.

The place in which Cary found himself as a writer now becomes clear.
In order to be true to his perception of reality, he had to construct his
novels as works of art giving only a partial picture of the truth. He could
never allow himself to depict a character, as Hardy had done with Tess,
who has an ultimate or fixed truth. His presentation, he believed, could
never be more than partial, the scope of his fictive vision limited by the
form of the novel. Chester Nimmo, Cock Jarvis, Gulley Jimson, Rudbeck, and all the other powerful characters in the pantheon of his art
must remain ambiguous. We are never to be allowed to say of them,
"This is a bad man; this, a good woman. Here the forces of good have
triumphed; there, the forces of evil." Cary will remain true to his
conviction and compel us to see his world as he saw it, incomplete and
only partially perceived, its truth revealed in the ambivalent symbol of
his art.

Aside from his critical writing, Cary produced a substantial body of
political commentary with its major points of focus being Africa and the
role of freedom in politics. It would require a book to deal in any detail
with the mass of this writing, but two works, *The Case for African
Freedom* and *Process of Real Freedom,* provide clear indications of the
direction and color of Cary's thought. Characteristically, Cary's political
stance too derives from his conviction that men are born free and require
freedom to achieve moral and spiritual fulfillment.

The Case for African Freedom

Having spent nearly ten years in Africa as a soldier and civil servant,
Cary quite naturally felt himself uniquely qualified to write on the
African question, as it began to emerge in the 1930s and 1940s, heated
up by the onset of World War II.

The Case for African Freedom, by its title, makes clear Cary's basic
position on the issue of political independence for the client states on the
African continent. His argument is both pragmatic and idealistic. That
is to say, he grounds his conviction that the African colonies should be
moved toward nationhood on two premises, that mankind is "driving
toward the same goal, the realization of its own personal powers, its own
unique freedom . . . ,"[2] and that the only security any government can

finally count on is being on the side of freedom (*AF,* 136). More practically, Cary says that freedom is bound to come to the African states. Let us make sure they are equipped to make their governments work.

Gradualism is also a part of Cary's argument. He urges a period of transition, in which black Africans are given a larger share of government responsibility until they are equipped to carry on on their own. "Revolution [Cary's word for independence] by itself would lead to disaster for the African masses," he writes and insists on the point over and over again. In terms of the recent history of some of the black African states, it would be difficult to deny the wisdom of Cary's assessment. Unfortunately, the white incumbents were unwilling to allow the black African into positions of power. The liberation movements in Africa have been compelled, in ways not even Cary envisioned, to resort to force to assume control of their own political destinies.

Despite his years of experience in the colonial service, Cary still found it possible to write that "the purpose laid down from the beginning, through all forms of British colonial government, direct and indirect, has actually been, at least in theory, to prepare the dependent peoples for self-government" (*AF,* 49). Perhaps the "at least in theory" gives Cary a means of escaping the charge of, at best, naiveté and, at worst, dishonesty. It is certainly not the view of Leonard Woolf and George Orwell, both of whom were also colonial administrators.

Perhaps Cary believed what he had written about the aims of British colonialism. He certainly believed that "European conquest, with all its faults, [had] brought incomparably more good than harm to Africa" (*AF,* 19). He was thinking, of course, of medicine, roads, a breaking up of the chiefs' and witch doctors' tyrannical grip on the tribes, and the possibilities for growth offered by Western style education and technical training. It is perplexing, however, to find the author of *Mister Johnson* making such a statement. It is fair to say that not a single one of Cary's African novels show the Westernization of the African lands to be anything other than a disaster for the African people. Death and disintegration follow on the heels of the white man's arrival. The cultures are shattered, the way of life disrupted, the lands expropriated, and the people's very lives put into jeopardy. But if Cary spoke with a divided voice, it is almost certainly because he was unaware of the contradiction. The artist and the thinker appear to have seen Africa through different eyes.

The Process of Real Freedom

Published in 1943, when some of the darkness of the war had begun to disperse, *The Process of Real Freedom* was aimed at those elements in British political life and, perhaps, in the United States as well, that had begun to express the fear that the democracies had utterly failed, that World War II was the final proof of that failure. Cary wrote to counter this feeling.

He begins his argument by saying that the democracies were right to resist Germany and Japan with force. "Men," he writes, "may agree to differ on matters of taste or custom, they will come to an understanding on economic questions, but when their conscience is touched they are bound in honour to fight, to risk their lives."[3] And he follows this assertion with the observation that rather than diminish, the causes of war are certain to increase, "as propaganda spreads abroad new ideas, new reasons of difference between men, new knowledge of differences which already exist" (*RF,* 3).

Cary defends democracy as the logical outgrowth of man's desire to control his own political affairs and to come to some sort of outward recognition of the basic reality in human existence, that each of us possesses a unique individuality, a distinct consciousness, and a compelling responsibility to act in accordance with our freedom. He then defines "real" freedom as "a man's power to do what he likes; that is to say, to form his own ideas, his own purpose" (*RF,* 7).

Cary regards the movement toward a political democracy to be world wide. Even among the nations under the thumb of tyrannies, he finds the tendency toward political self-expression making its way forward. The source of his optimism is twofold. First, he considered it to be in man's inherent nature to be free. Cary's phrase, "Freedom was born without a name" (*RF,* 9), means that freedom is a constant in human destiny, is not identified with sect or party, and is a part of man's creative power. Second, political freedom follows on the heels of the creation of skilled workers. Once a man learns a craft, the situation is brought into being that will propel him inevitably toward self-expression in his political life. He will ultimately insist on participating in his own political destiny.

Given Cary's conviction that history is not a merry-go-round but a progression and that man is a part of that progression, the political writings inevitably take on a distinctive coloration. Freedom, Cary's great theme, is the reality within which creation has its being. Everything moves forward. As he goes ahead he finds himself confronted with his own freedom, burdened with it, if you will, but certainly defined by it. With the burden and glory of this freedom comes another burden, responsibility. In taking up this responsibility man must, Cary insists, become responsible for his own political destiny. And in becoming responsible in this fashion, he must evolve a democratic system. Cary was a fatalist, and the agent of destiny in his compelling vision is freedom.

Chapter Eleven
In Conclusion

To place Cary among the other novelists of his period is to see how highly differentiated his brand of fiction is. In some respects, of course, he maintained the tradition of the novel. He was profoundly middle class in his preoccupation with respectability. That this preoccupation is expressed in opposition, such as Gulley Jimson's struggle against the forces of order in his world, against the Beeders' wealth, Hickson's conservatism, and Sara's desire for a first class funeral, only serves to underline his obsession. In every novel from *Aissa Saved* to *The Captive and the Free* the broad foundations of his fictive worlds are built on the middle-class values of order, respectability, moral responsibility, and conventional values.

Over and over again his protagonists come to grief against the adamantine walls of propriety, social conservatism, and cultural Philistinism. But he is not, like Aldous Huxley in such novels as *Point Counter Point,* a social satirist. Even in his political trilogy he is not a political novelist in the sense that George Orwell is in *1984* or *Burmese Days.* In his African stories Cary is not primarily concerned to show the major configurations of African life as Leonard Woolf sets out to do in *The Village And The Jungle.* The closest he comes to writing this sort of novel of cultural exploration is in *Castle Corner,* an attempt that was only partially successful. One has only to mention such writers as Thomas Hardy, Arnold Bennett, and John Galsworthy to understand how different was the flow of Cary's artistic genius.

Neither can it be said that Cary was a particularly experimental writer. His occasional excursions into the use of the first person or any of the minor structural experiments in his novels are modest efforts. Considering the work of Conrad, Ford, and Joyce, who came before him, or that of Samuel Beckett, a contemporary, or Henry Green and Ivy Compton-Burnett, one can see that Cary obviously was not primarily interested in remaking the form of the novel. There is little in Cary's novels that would appear strange, so far as form is concerned, to a

ninteenth-century reader, especially one familiar with George Meredith or
Laurence Sterne.

He is quite different from a chronicler of English life like Anthony
Powell in his *Music of Time* series or C. P. Snow who, in his *Strangers And
Brothers* novels, strives to explain the grave dangers to our society posed
by the division between scientist and nonscientist. One can read all of
Cary's novels without encountering an overview of English life. This is
not to say that one does not encounter vivid and memorable renderings of
English and Irish life in Cary's novels. Chester Nimmo's childhood, life
at Castle Corner, Gulley Jimson's London are only a few examples of the
vitality of Cary's ability to convey a sense of place and time. But such
effects, powerful as they may be, are not the heart of his fiction.

Does he, then, belong to any tradition in English literature? The
answer is yes, but it is not one closely of his time. From the time of
William Langland in the fourteenth century onward, there have appeared at intervals writers whose work has been the product of intense
and powerfully compelling visions of reality. Langland's *Piers the Plowman* is an early example of the type and John Bunyan's *The Pilgrim's
Progress* is another. It may seem strange to compare Cary to Langland and
Bunyan, but the strangeness is soon overcome when one begins to think
about the sources of their inspiration.

William Blake, Bunyan, Langland, and others of their kind wrote out
of a conviction that they had encountered the truth and were God-bound
to reveal it. A modern reader may be made uncomfortable by a close
encounter with a writer claiming to be a voice from the horse's mouth,
but that is only because he no longer lives in an age of faith. Even Cary's
vision, when it came to him, came in a secular revelation that he called
truth and not God. Still, his vision was of such force that it accounts for
the shape of his art and, indeed, all of his life thereafter.

Cary believed that he had discovered the fundamental truth about
human existence. This truth reveals man condemned to freedom in a
universe that is constantly changing. The nature of the change is that the
old is broken up to make way for the new and that the only way the new
can be formed is through the destruction of the old. All attempts to
preserve anything, whether it is a custom or a castle, is doomed to
failure. Nothing survives. Everything changes; and man must, as long as
he lives, continuously make choices in his life that cause him to change
also. In this sense Cary's universe is fated.

Such a view of things might, conceivably, have led Cary to preach a
stoic indifference toward the monstrousness of life. But his vision led
him, in fact, in quite another direction. The freedom that man has had

thrust upon him allows him to shape his own life. This is regarded by Cary as a great opportunity for man to develop his moral nature. Of course it also provides him, as well, with the opportunity to develop the satanic aspect of his nature.

The characters in Cary's fiction are often engaged in the task of building their souls. The problem is that this development does not go on smoothly. Tempted by greed, selfishness, power, and complacency, characters backslide, go sideways, and fall from grace. Even the best of Cary's characters fail to avoid all of the pitfalls laid in their paths. Aissa runs away from the mission to be with her lover. Jim Lattimer becomes a murderer. Chester Nimmo cannot resist the attractions of power. Sara Monday constantly surprises herself with her failures.

The worlds that Cary creates in his novels are also systematically destroyed. In the African novels, the native culture is ploughed up and the tribes broken. In *The Horse's Mouth,* the wall on which Gulley paints his last picture is bulldozed into rubble. The Corner house goes out of the family. In *To Be A Pilgrim* Wilcher cannot prevent Tolbrook from being wrecked or Tenacre from being stripped of its trees and hedges and ploughed into a faceless field, where machines can labor unimpeded by lanes or copses or laborers' cottages. In the novels nothing remains unchanged.

In this chaos has Cary found any abiding values? Several. They are all connected with the way in which people deal with one another. Clearly, family life was important to Cary. It can be seen in his own personal history as well as in its representation in his work. It is particularly evident in his evocation of childhood in *Charley is My Darling, Castle Corner, A House of Children, Prisoner of Grace,* and elsewhere. Children in particular in his fiction are sustained by love and harmed by its absence.

Love among the adults in his novels tends to run to a formula. Cary's women are victims or tyrants. And the clear implication is that women who are not suppressed, by physical force if necessary, will become tyrants. His view of women is, in my opinion, the least appealing part of his comprehensive vision. His men are either creators such as Mister Johnson and Gulley Jimson who destroy the old world, or conservative men such as Hickson, Lattimer, and Wilcher who vainly strive to maintain the old world. Cary's women love both varieties of men and are often ground between them.

Today, Cary has lost much of the popularity that he worked so arduously to win. He certainly qualifies for the epithet of neglected writer. To be great, a writer must demonstrate a breadth of vision and a universality of appeal that will make him accessible and attractive to a wide range of readers. He must both be of his time and transcend his time. He must be copious enough to have created in his work a picture of the world that is rich and complex. He must give a clear vision of life. He must be a consummate storyteller.

By these measures Cary is a great novelist. He meets every condition set down. He is neglected, perhaps, because in the last analysis readers demand to hear what the great myths and the lowly folk tales tell them, that life is a struggle between life and death and that life wins. In Cary's novels the struggle ends in a draw.

It is quite possible to point out that, over and over again in European literature, we find life being defeated. In Ibsen, Zola, Flaubert, the reader sees the dream crushed, the blossom blown. Indeed, the blossom can be observed withering in Hardy's *Jude The Obscure* and in *Tess*. But Hardy is an exception. In the tradition, of the English novel, from Defoe to Iris Murdoch, life wins. Evil is cast out like winter's garment to be burned in the purifying flame of spring's rebirth.

Cary does not give his readers that ritual cleansing, but he gives them much else. His novels are brimming with life, the lines dance with energy, and his characters have sufficient force to march, frequently, straight off the page into our memories. Gulley Jimson, to name only one, is a permanent addition to English literature's pantheon of fictional immortals. Cary was a great writer and a great visionary. The neglect which now afflicts his work will be amended, and he will once again be brought forward to stand in the first rank of English novelists.

Notes and References

Preface

1. Robert Bloom, *The Indeterminate World: A Study of The Novels of Joyce Cary* (Philadelphia, 1962).

Chapter One

1. Malcomb Foster, *Joyce Cary: A Biography* (Boston, 1968), p. 11.
2. Ibid., p. 12.
3. Ibid., p. 21.
4. Ibid., p. 29.
5. Ibid., p. 30.
6. Ibid., p. 43.
7. Ibid., p. 227.
8. Ibid., p. 332.
9. Ibid., p. 365.
10. Ibid., p. 411.
11. Ibid., p. 452.
12. Ibid., p. 436.
13. Ibid., p. 463.
14. Ibid., p. 494.
15. Ibid., p. 495.

Chapter Two

1. Enid Starkie, "Joyce Cary: A Personal Portrait," *Virginia Quarterly Review* 37 ( ):110–34.
2. Foster, *Joyce Cary*, p. 126.
3. Ibid., p. 129.
4. Joyce Cary, *Cock Jarvis*, ed. A. G. Bishop (New York, 1947), p. ix; hereafter cited in the text as *CJ*.
5. Foster, *Joyce Cary*, p. 113.
6. M. M. Mahood, *Joyce Cary's Africa* (Boston, 1964), p. 40.
7. Foster, *Joyce Cary*, p. 135.
8. Mahood, *Joyce Cary's Africa*, p. 59.
9. Ibid.
10. Ibid., p. 60.

11. Foster, *Joyce Cary,* p. 128.

12. Mahood, *Joyce Cary's Africa,* p. 61.

13. Foster, *Joyce Cary,* p. 230.

14. Mahood, *Joyce Cary's Africa,* p. 63.

15. Foster, *Joyce Cary,* p. 235.

16. Ibid., p. 238.

17. Ibid., p. 246.

18. Joyce Cary, *Aissa Saved* (New York, 1963), p. 218; hereafter cited in the text as *AS.*

19. Joyce Cary, Author's Note, in *Mister Johnson* (New York, 1951), p. 261; hereafter cited in the text as *MJ.*

Chapter Three

1. Mahood, *Joyce Cary's Africa,* p. 95.

2. Ibid., p. 89.

3. Ibid., p. 95.

4. Joyce Cary, *An American Visitor* (New York, 1961), p. 91; hereafter cited in the text as *AV.*

5. Mahood, *Joyce Cary's Africa,* pp. 126–27.

6. Ibid., p. 130.

7. Foster, *Joyce Cary,* pp: 291–92.

8. Golden L. Larson, *The Dark Descent: Social Change and Moral Responsibility in the Novels of Joyce Cary* (London, 1965), p. 27.

9. Joyce Cary, *The African Witch* (New York, 1962), p. 311; hereafter cited in the text as *AW.*

10. Bloom, *Indeterminate World,* p. 54.

11. Arnold Kettle, *An Introduction to The English Novel* (New York: Harper & Row, 1960), 2:83.

12. Bloom, *Indeterminate World,* p. 58.

13. Andrew Wright, *Joyce Cary: A Preface to His Novels* (New York, 1958), p. 86.

14. Bloom, *Indeterminate World,* p. 58.

Chapter Four

1. Wright, *Joyce Cary,* p. 62.

2. Ibid., p. 63.

3. Larson, *Dark Descent,* p. 101.

4. Foster, *Joyce Cary,* p. 338.

5. Joyce Cary, *A House of Children* (New York, 1956), p. 4; hereafter cited in the text as *HC.*

6. Joyce Cary, *Charley is My Darling* (London, 1956), p. 83; hereafter cited in the text as *CD.*

7. Cary, Prefatory Essay, in ibid., unpaged.

8. Ibid.
9. Foster, *Joyce Cary,* p. 339.
10. Ibid., p. 346.
11. Wright, *Joyce Cary,* p. 63.
12. Bloom, *Indeterminate World,* pp. 323–25.
13. Foster, *Joyce Cary,* p. 351.
14. Ibid., p. 351.
15. Ibid., p. 502.
16. Ibid., p. 222.
17. Bloom, *Indeterminate World,* p. 63.
18. Ibid., p. 63.

Chapter Five

1. Joyce Cary, *Castle Corner* (London, 1960), p. 7; hereafter cited in the text as *CC.*
2. Foster, *Joyce Cary,* pp. 312–13.
3. Ibid., p. 352.
4. Larson, *Dark Descent,* p. 183.
5. Foster, *Joyce Cary,* p. 428.
6. Joyce Cary, *A Fearful Joy* (New York, 1963), p. 8; hereafter cited in the text as *FJ.*
7. Wright, *Joyce Cary,* p. 69.
8. Ibid., p. 66.
9. Foster, *Joyce Cary,* pp. 212–13.
10. Stanley Weintraub, *"Castle Corner:* Joyce Cary's Buddenbrooks," *Wisconsin Studies in Contemporary Literature* 5 (Winter–Spring 1964):54–63.
11. Joyce Cary, *The Moonlight* (New York, 1946), p. 11; hereafter cited in the text as *M.*
12. Larson, *Dark Descent,* p. 182.
13. R. W. Noble, *Joyce Cary* (New York, 1973), p. 16.
14. Foster, *Joyce Cary,* p. 428.

Chapter Six

1. Foster, *Joyce Cary,* p. 345.
2. Ibid., p. 365.
3. Joyce Cary, *Herself Surprised,* in *First Trilogy* (New York, 1958), p. 2; hereafter cited in the text as *HS.*
4. Joyce Cary, *To Be A Pilgrim,* in *First Trilogy* (New York, 1958), p. 3; hereafter cited in the text as *P.*
5. Bloom, *Indeterminate World,* p. 86.
6. Wright, *Joyce Cary,* p. 119.
7. Joyce Cary, *The Horse's Mouth,* in *First Trilogy* (New York, 1958), p. 284; hereafter cited in the text as *HM.*

8. Foster, *Joyce Cary*, p. 382.

9. Ibid., p. 381.

10. Giles Mitchell, *The Art Theme in Joyce Cary's First Trilogy* (The Hague, 1971), p. 23.

11. Bloom, *Indeterminate World*, p. 96.

12. Mitchell, *Art Theme*, p. 57.

13. Ibid., p. 53.

14. See also ibid., p. 71.

15. Ibid., p. 59.

16. Foster, *Joyce Cary*, pp. 365–67.

17. Ibid.

18. Ibid., p. 375.

19. Cary, *First Trilogy*, p. xiv.

20. Mitchell, *Art Theme*, p. 90.

21. Ibid., p. 93.

22. Ibid., p. 92.

23. Ibid., p. 107–8.

Chapter Seven

1. Foster, *Joyce Cary*, p. 419.

2. Joyce Cary, *Prisoner of Grace* (New York, 1952), p. 300; hereafter cited in the text as *PG*.

3. Jack Wolkenfeld, *Joyce Cary: The Developing Style* (New York, 1968), p. 180.

4. Joyce Cary, *Except The Lord* (New York, 1953), p. 83; hereafter cited in the text as *EL*.

5. Barbara Fisher, *Joyce Cary: The Writer And His Theme* (London, 1980), p. 281.

6. Ibid., p. 268.

7. Bloom, *Indeterminate World*, p. 140.

8. M. J. C. Echeruo, *Joyce Cary And The Novel of Africa* (New York, 1972), p. 123.

9. Joyce Cary, *Not Honour More* (New York, 1955), p. 32.

10. Fisher, *Joyce Cary*, p. 294.

11. Foster, *Joyce Cary*, p. 473.

12. Ibid., p. 475.

13. Fisher, *Joyce Cary*, p. 277.

Chapter Eight

1. Wright, *Joyce Cary*, p. 50.

2. Joyce Cary, *The Captive and the Free*, ed. Winifred Davin (New York, 1959), p. 367; hereafter cited in the text as *C*.

3. Larsen, *Dark Descent,* p. 192.
4. Foster, *Joyce Cary,* p. 506.
5. Bloom, *Indeterminate World,* p. 105.
6. Ibid.
7. Fisher, *Joyce Cary,* p. 307.
8. Ibid., p. 308.

Chapter Nine

1. Foster, *Joyce Cary,* p. 231.
2. Ibid.
3. Wright, *Joyce Cary,* p. 7.
4. Ibid., p. 45.

Chapter Ten

1. Joyce Cary, *Art and Reality: Ways of the Creative Process* (New York, 1958), p. 18; hereafter cited in the text as *AR.*
2. Joyce Cary, *The Case for African Freedom And Other Writings on Africa* (Austin, Texas, 1962), p. 51; hereafter cited in the text as *AF.*
3. Joyce Cary, *The Process of Real Freedom* (London, 1943), p. 3; hereafter cited in the text as *RF.*

Selected Bibliography

PRIMARY SOURCES

1. Books

Verse. [Arthur Cary, pseud.]. Edinburgh: Robert Grant, July 1908.
Aissa Saved. London: Ernest Benn, 1932.
An American Visitor. London: Ernest Benn, 1933.
The African Witch. London: Victor Gollancz, 1936.
Castle Corner. London: Victor Gollancz, 1938.
Power in Men. London: Nicholson & Watson, 1939.
Mister Johnson. London: Victor Gollancz, 1939.
Charley is My Darling. London: Michael Joseph, 1940.
A House of Children. London: Michael Joseph, 1941.
The Case for African Freedom. London: Secker & Warburg, 1941.
Herself Surprised. London: Michael Joseph, 1941.
To Be a Pilgrim. London: Michael Joseph, 1942.
Process of Real Freedom. London: Michael Joseph, 1943.
The Horse's Mouth. London: Michael Joseph, 1944.
Marching Soldier. London: Michael Joseph, 1945. Poetry.
The Moonlight. London: Michael Joseph, 1946.
Britain and West Africa. London: Longmans, Green, 1946.
The Drunken Sailor: A Ballad-Epic. London: Michael Joseph, 1947.
A Fearful Joy. London: Michael Joseph, 1949.
Prisoner of Grace. London: Michael Joseph, 1952.
Except the Lord. London: Michael Joseph, 1953.
Not Honour More. London: Michael Joseph, 1955.
Art and Reality. Cambridge: At the University Press, 1958.
The Captive and the Free. London: Michael Joseph, 1959.
Spring Song and Other Stories. London: Michael Joseph, 1960.
Memoir of the Bobotes. Austin: University of Texas Press, 1960.
Cock Jarvis an Unfinished Novel. Edited by A. G. Bishop. London: Michael
    Joseph, 1974.
Selected Essays. Edited by A. G. Bishop. London: Michael Joseph, 1976.

2. Short Stories and Articles

"Lombrosine." [Thomas Joyce, pseud.]. *Saturday Evening Post*, 31 January 1920, pp. 30, 32, 62.

"The Springs of Youth." [Thomas Joyce, pseud.]. *Saturday Evening Post*, 6 March 1920, pp. 30, 32, 189, 190.

"The Idealist." [Thomas Joyce, pseud.]. *Saturday Evening Post*, 13 March 1920, pp. 40, 42.

"The Cure." [Thomas Joyce, pseud.]. *Saturday Evening Post*, 1 May 1920, pp. 30, 99.

"The Reformation." [Thomas Joyce, pseud.]. *Saturday Evening Post*, 22 May 1920, pp. 20, 21, 124.

"A Piece of Honesty." [Thomas Joyce, pseud.]. *Saturday Evening Post*, 26 June 1920, pp. 66, 69, 70.

"The Bad Samaritan." [Thomas Joyce, pseud.]. *Saturday Evening Post*, 3 July 1920, pp. 40, 42, 44, 46.

"A Consistent Woman." [Thomas Joyce, pseud.]. *Saturday Evening Post*, 21 August 1920, pp. 30, 32, 81, 82.

"None But the Brave." [Thomas Joyce, pseud.]. *Saturday Evening Post*, 11 September 1920, pp. 18, 19, 100.

"Salute to Propriety." [Thomas Joyce, pseud.]. *Saturday Evening Post*, 9 October 1920, pp. 40, 42, 45, 46.

"'On the Line' An Academy Story." [T. Joyce, pseud.]. *Strand Magazine* 61 (May 1921):454–60.

"The Uncle." [Thomas Joyce, pseud.]. *Hutchinson's Magazine* 4 (June 1921):601–15.

"The Failure." [T. Joyce, pseud.]. *Strand Magazine* 62 (October 1921):369–77.

"Not Wholly Matrimony." [Thomas Joyce, pseud.]. *Strand Magazine* 66 (December 1923):655–65.

"Bush River." *Windmill* 1, no. 2 (1945):120–25.

"The Way a Novel Gets Written." *Harper's Magazine* 200 (February 1950):87–93.

"Umaru." *Cornhill Magazine* 165 (Winter 1950–51):50–54.

"The Novelist at Work: A Conversation Between Joyce Cary and Lord David Cecil." *Adam International Review* 18, nos. 212–13 (November–December 1950):15–25.

"Success Story." *Harper's Magazine* 204 (June 1952):74–76.

"Evangelist." *Harper's Magazine* 205 (November 1952):88–89.

"Buying a Horse." *Punch*, 2 December 1953, pp. 654–56.

"Spring Song." *London Magazine* 1 (March 1954):29–31.

"The Limit." *Esquire* 41 (June 1954):43.

"A Good Investment." *Harper's Magazine* 209 (December 1954):64–72.

"Carmagnole." *London Magazine* 2 (February 1955):37–39.

"A Glory of the Moon." *Mademoiselle* 41 (May 1955):101, 156.

"The Breakout." *New Yorker*, 2 February 1957, pp. 28–36.
"New Boots." *Harper's Bazaar* 55 (March 1957):92–93, 117, 126.
"Psychologist." *Harper's Bazaar* 90 (May 1957):140–42, 175–80, 182, 185.
"The Tunnel." *Vogue* 130 (1 October 1957):186, 187, 226.
"Happy Marriage." *Harper's Magazine* 216 (April 1958):65–68.
"Period Piece." *Harper's Bazaar*, April 1958, pp. 110, 111, 208.
"A Hero of Our Time." *London Magazine* 5 (September 1958):13–18.
"The Sheep." *Texas Quarterly* 1, no. 4 (Winter 1958):23–37.
"A Government Baby." *Lilliput* 44 (July 1959):13, 14, 18, 62–65.

SECONDARY SOURCES

1. Books

Allen, Walter Ernest. *Writers and Their Work*. Revised ed. London: Longmans, Green & Co., 1963. Helpful, brief introduction to the writer.

Bloom, Robert. *The Intermediate World: A Study of the Novels of Joyce Cary*. Philadelphia: University of Pennsylvania Press, 1962. Detailed examination of moral indefiniteness in the novels of Joyce Cary. An important study.

Echeruo, M. J. C. *Joyce Cary and the Novel of Africa*. New York: Africana Publishing Co., 1972. Helpful guide to the African background.

————. *Joyce Cary and the Dimensions of Order*. New York: Barnes and Noble, 1979. Very useful on the political trilogy.

Fisher, Barbara. *Joyce Cary: The Writer and his Theme*. London: Colin Smythe, 1980. Excellent study of the life and work with special emphasis on the people and experiences that influenced Cary's art.

Foster, Malcomb. *Joyce Cary: A Biography*. Boston: Houghton Mifflin, 1968. Excellent introduction to the life.

Hoffman, Charles G. *Joyce Cary: The Comedy of Freedom*. Pittsburg: University of Pittsburg Press, 1964. Useful guide to the fiction.

Kanu, S. H. *A World of Everlasting Conflict: Joyce Cary's View of Man and Society*. Ibadan, Nigeria: Ibadan University Press, 1974. A study of Cary's view of creation as flux.

Larsen, Golden L. *The Dark Descent: Social Change and Moral Responsibility in the Novels of Joyce Cary*. London: Michael Joseph, 1965. A thoughtful and valuable exploration of Cary's social and moral visions as they are worked out in the fiction.

Mahood, M. M. *Joyce Cary's Africa*. London: Camelot Press, 1964. An indispensable guide to the African fiction.

Mitchell, Giles. *The Art Theme in Joyce Cary's First Trilogy*. The Hague: Mouton, 1971. Important examination and analysis of the art theme in the trilogy.

Noble, R. W. *Joyce Cary.* New York: Barnes and Noble, 1973. Useful introductory work to the writer.

Soderskog, Ingvar. *Joyce Cary's "Hard Conceptual Labour"; A Structural Analysis of To Be A Pilgrim.* Gothenburg: Acta University Gothoburgensis, 1977. The title describes the work.

Wolkenfeld, Jack. *Joyce Cary: The Developing Style.* New York: New York University Press, 1968. Important study of Cary's writing techniques.

Wright, Andrew. *Joyce Cary: A Preface to His Novels.* London: Chatto & Windus, 1958. An early study of the writer that is still valuable. One of the best introductory studies yet written.

2. Articles

Adam International Review 18 (November–December 1950). The issue is devoted to Joyce Cary. A good source for current critical attitudes.

Adams, Hazard. "The Three Speakers of Joyce Cary." *Modern Fiction Studies* 5 (Summer 1959):108–20. Helpful in analyzing Cary's narrative voices.

————. "Blake and Gulley Jimson: English Symbolists." *Critique* 3 (Spring–Fall 1959):3–14. Interesting and intelligent comparison.

Allen, Walter. "A Flood of Memories." *New York Times Book Review,* 4 March 1956, p. 6.

Battaglia, Francis Joseph. "Spurious Armageddon: Joyce Cary's *Not Honour More.*" *Modern Fiction Studies* 13 (Winter 1967–68):479–91. A useful critical introduction to the novels.

Bettman, Elizabeth R. "Joyce Cary And The Problem of Political Morality." *Antioch Review* 17 (Summer 1957):266–72. Valuable background to the political novels.

Brown, Patricia. "Creative Losers: Blacks, Children And Women in The Novels of Joyce Cary." *DAI* 34:6627A (MA), 1974. Very important study of a neglected aspect of Cary's work.

Cary, Edward. "The Free World of Joyce Cary." *Modern Age* 3 (Spring 1959):115–24. A look at Cary's moral stance.

Cecil, Lord David. "The Novelist At Work: A Conversation Between Joyce Cary And Lord David Cecil." *Adam International Review* 18 (November–December 1950):15–25. A glimpse of Cary's approach to writing.

Cohen, Nathan. "A Conversation with Joyce Cary." *Tamarack Review* 3 (Spring 1957):5–15. Informative view of Cary as writer.

Cowley, Malcomb. *Writers At Work: The Paris Review Interviews.* New York: Viking Press, 1958, pp. 51–67. Outstanding interview.

Davin, Dan. "Five Windows Darken: Recollections of Joyce Cary." *Encounter,* June 1975, pp. 24–33. Interesting personal recollection.

Fisher, Barbara. "Joyce Cary's Published Writings." *Bodleian Library Record* 8, no. 4 (April 1970):213–28. This material covered more fully in Fisher's book-length study.

Galligan, Edward. "Intuition And Concept: Joyce Cary And The Critics." *Texas Studies in Literature And Language* 8 (1967):81–87. A useful exploration of Cary's critical reception.

Gardener, Helen. "The Novels of Joyce Cary." *Essays And Studies by Members of The English Association* 28 (1975):76–93. A reliable guide.

Garrett. "The Major Poetry of Joyce Cary." *Modern Fiction Studies* 9 (Autumn 1963):245–56. Deals with a neglected aspect of Cary's work.

Hardy, Barbara, "Form in Joyce Cary's Novels." *Essays in Criticism* 4 (April 1954):180–90. Useful introduction to the subject.

Hoffmann, Charles G. "Joyce Cary And The Comic Mask." *Western Humanities Review* 13 (Spring 1959):135–42.

————. "The Captive And The Free: Joyce Cary's Unfinished Trilogy." *Texas Studies in English Literature And Language* 5 (Spring 1963):17–24.

————. "The Genesis And Development of Joyce Cary's First Trilogy." *PMLA* 78 (September 1963):431–39. Hoffman's pieces are all informative, reliable introductory studies.

Jan Mohamed, Abdul R. *Joyce Cary's African Romances.* Working Papers, no. 5 Brookline, Mass.: Boston University, African Studies Center, 1978. An interesting perspective on the African novels.

Johnson, Pamela Hansford. "Three Novelists And The Drawing of Character: C. P. Snow, Joyce Cary, and Ivy Compton-Burnett." *Essays and Studies by Members of the English Association* (London: n.p., 1950), pp. 82–91. Perceptive view of Cary by a fellow novelist.

Karl, Frederick R. "Joyce Cary: The Moralist As Novelist." *Twentieth Century Literature* 5 (January 1960): 183–96.

Meriwether, James B. "The Books of Joyce Cary: A Preliminary Bibliography of English And American Editions." *Texas Studies in English Literature And Language* 1 (Summer 1959):300–310.

Salz, Paulina J. "The Philosophical Principles in Joyce Cary's Work." *Western Humanities Review* 20 (Spring 1966): 159–65.

Schorer, Mark. "The Socially Extensive Novel." *Adam International Review* 18 (November–December 1950):31–32. Ties Cary to the tradition of social realism.

Starkie, Enid. "Joyce Cary: A Portrait." In *Essays by Divers Hands,* edited by Joanna Richardson. London: Oxford University Press, 1963, pp. 124–44. A revealing personal recollection.

Stevenson, Lionel. "Joyce Cary and The Anglo-Irish Tradition." *Modern Fiction Studies* 9 (Autumn 1963):210–16.

Stockholder, Fred. "The Triple Vision of Joyce Cary's First Trilogy." *Modern Fiction Studies* 9 (Autumn 1963):231–44. A thoughtful study.

Wells, Glenn Lawrence, Jr. "The Role of the Female in Relation to The Artist in The Works of Joyce Cary." *DAI* 36:4521A. Essential for a thorough study of the issues involved.

Telling, John. "Joyce Cary's Moral World." *Modern Fiction Studies* 9 (Autumn 1963):276–83. Good background to the novels.

Wright, Andrew. "Joyce Cary's Unpublished Work." *London Magazine* 5 (January 1958):35–42. A unique account.

————. "An Authoritative Text of *The Horse's Mouth.*" *Papers of The Bibliographical Society of America* 61 (2d Quarter 1967):100–109.

Index

134

DATE DUE

DEMCO 38-297